Words of Life

The Bible Day by Day
September–December 2011

HODDER &
STOUGHTON

First published in Great Britain in 2011 by Hodder & Stoughton
An Hachette UK company

A CIP catalogue record for this title is available from the British Library

ISBN 978 1 444 70134 0

Typeset in Plantin Light by Avon DataSet Ltd, Bidford on Avon, Warwickshire

Printed and bound in Great Britain
by Clays Ltd, St Ives plc

Hodder & Stoughton policy is to use papers that are natural, renewable
and recyclable products and made from wood grown in sustainable forests.
The logging and manufacturing processes are expected to conform to the
environmental regulations of the country of origin.

Hodder & Stoughton Ltd
338 Euston Road
London NW1 3BH

www.hodderfaith.com

Contents

From the Literary Secretary

Life is full of transitions. Every day we grow in our understanding and adjust our thoughts, beliefs and actions accordingly. Transitions are a result of beginnings and endings. This volume of *Words of Life* is a transition edition. It is the book between the writings of Major Evelyn Merriam (who has concluded her assignment as writer of *Words of Life*) and Major Beverly Ivany (who is to be the new writer).

In compiling this transition edition, the Assistant Literary Secretary, Major Trevor Howes, has brought together a variety of thought-provoking and challenging devotional writings. Major Ivany is introduced through two mini-series, one focusing on the simple cup as a symbol of life and the other a post-Christmas series leading into the new year. In his Advent series, guest writer Lieutenant-Colonel André Sterckx helps us to understand how God came to earth for our salvation, in the person of Jesus Christ.

The remainder of this volume comes from previously published books by Salvationist writers which, in the main, endeavour to unpack various aspects of the purpose and personality of Jesus Christ. Excerpts from *100 Portraits of Christ* provide insights into the person and ministry of Christ, as revealed by the names and titles ascribed to him in Scripture. A series collated from *Holiness Unwrapped* presents Jesus as both the example and spiritual source for holy living.

The fruit of the Spirit is the focus of a series adapted from a chapter of *Never the Same Again* – a helpful guide to the walk of faith for new Christians and for others desiring to revisit the foundations of faith. *Question Time* brings insights into Jesus' teaching on citizenship in the kingdom of God as recorded in Matthew's Gospel. The focus is on questions asked by Jesus, his disciples and the Jewish and Roman authorities.

Readings for Sundays are from two books, *Stories That Are Seen* and *More Stories That Are Seen*, which use parables of Jesus to reveal how even today they still have power to positively impact our daily living.

Lieutenant-Colonel Laurie Robertson
International Headquarters, London

Abbreviations

AB	*Amplified Bible* © 1965, Zondervan.
GNB	*Good News Bible* © 1994 Bible Societies/HarperCollins Publishers Ltd.
JBP	*The New Testament in Modern English*, J. B. Phillips, Geoffrey Bles. © J. B. Phillips, 1958, 1959, 1960, 1972. HarperCollins Publishers.
JMT	*James Moffat Translation* © 1922, 1924, 1925, 1926, 1935. HarperCollins Publishers.
KJV	*King James Bible* (Authorised Version).
MSG	*The Message*, Eugene H. Peterson. © 1993, 1994, 1995, 1996, 2000, 2001, 2002. Used by permission of NavPress Publishing Group.
NEB	*New English Bible* © 1961, 1970, Oxford University Press.
NKJV	*New King James Bible* © 1982 Thomas Nelson, Inc. Used by permission. All rights reserved.
REB	*Revised English Bible* © 1989, Cambridge University Press.
SASB	*The Song Book of The Salvation Army* © 1986 The General of The Salvation Army.
WB	*The New Testament, Volume 1*, William Barclay. © 1968, Collins, London, UK.

Portraits of Christ

The book 100 Portraits of Christ *is a biography of the person and ministry of Christ, as revealed by names and titles ascribed to him in Scripture. Written by Colonel Henry Gariepy, the collection was published in book form in 1987 by Scripture Press Publications Inc., USA, on behalf of The Salvation Army. A prolific and powerful author of Christian literature, Colonel Gariepy received The Salvation Army's highest honour for distinguished service when he was admitted to the Order of the Founder in June 2007. He was promoted to Glory in 2010.*

Introduction

Down through the centuries people have given meanings to names. In many cases, these meanings were suggestive of characteristics of that person. But today, we give little or no thought to the meanings of names and simply smile at the characteristics they suggest.

But quite the opposite is true of the names and titles of Jesus revealed in the Bible. These names were given by God not only to honour Christ but also to give us a clearer understanding of who he is. They give us a better grasp of his power, glory and greatness. Each name and title is a revealing portrait of our Lord, providing us with fresh insights and applications of their meaning for Christian living.

These brief studies of names and titles given to Jesus will undoubtedly enlarge our view of the Saviour and cause us to exclaim with the hymn-writer, 'How great thou art!'

Alpha and Omega

'I am the Alpha and the Omega' (v. 13).

This magnificent title of our Lord comes to us in his final words to man as recorded in the last chapter of the Bible. They are spoken in the context of his promise of the Second Coming. Three times in this final chapter he declares, 'I am coming soon!' (v. 12). The title Alpha and Omega gives authority and credibility to the stupendous promise of his return.

This title is found three times, each in the book of Revelation. They are believed to be the words of Jesus in 1:8 and the utterance of God the Father in 21:6.

Alpha and *omega* are words for the first and last letters of the Greek alphabet. Their meaning is explicit in the amplification Jesus himself gives in 22:13: 'The First and the Last, the Beginning and the End.'

He is *Alpha*, the Beginning, the First. What a staggering claim! First – before the empires of Egypt, Babylon, Greece, Rome. First – before the aeons of time spoken of by geologists. First – before the solar system, the Milky Way, the Pleiades.

He is *Omega*, the End, the Last. What a blessed assurance! Although Dante's great work was filled with tragedy, he entitled it *The Divine Comedy* because of his belief that in the end God would give happiness to his people.

As our Alpha and Omega, he is also the Lord of our beginnings and endings. He is there at the thresholds of our lives – birth, growing up, when the young person goes off to college, at the marriage altar, at the start of a career, when the first child comes, new undertakings, and all our important beginnings.

He is there in our endings – when we leave home, at the completion of a task, the end of a stay, leaving a place and friends behind, the loss of a loved one, retirement, death.

We take comfort and courage from this title with its assurance that our times are in the hands of the Eternal, our life becomes complete in him and he is the Lord of our beginning and endings.

Anointed One (Messiah)

*'Know and understand this: From the issuing of the decree to restore
and build Jerusalem until the Anointed One, the ruler, comes,
there will be seven "sevens", and sixty-two "sevens"' (v. 25).*

Bible characters are portrayed with brutal candour, 'warts and all'.
However, Daniel is one of the very few whose life is presented without
any faults. By then over eighty years of age, he was an elder statesman of
one of the world's great empires. His mind and heart were on the plight
of his people. Thinking of their exile and their destitute city and temple, he
was moved to a remarkable prayer of earnest intercession for his people
and their calamity.

How often God's answers and provisions exceed our askings! In answer
to his prayer, God gave Daniel a revelation of the coming Messiah, pertain-
ing not only to his coming but also to his chronology. If each 'week'
represents seven years we arrive at about AD 26, the time Jesus is believed
to have been baptised. But even more important were the *purposes* of his
coming, outlined in verses 24–27:

1. 'To finish transgression, to put an end to sin';
2. 'To atone for wickedness';
3. 'To bring in everlasting righteousness';
4. 'To seal up vision and prophecy' – all messianic prophecies would
   have their fulfilment in Christ;
5. 'To anoint the most holy' – Christ as the new 'Holy of holies' would
   replace the former tabernacle and temple mentioned in the prayer of
   Daniel;
6. The Messiah would be 'cut off' – a reference to his violent death;
7. Jerusalem would be destroyed by a great overflowing of war – a
   reference to its destruction in AD 70;
8. 'He will confirm a covenant with many';
9. 'He will put an end to sacrifice and suffering'.

All sacrifices were but types and foreshadowings of his great offering. His
death would end the period of legal sacrifices.

————

Prayer

Christ, satisfy the deepest longings and expectations of my heart and fulfil your
holy purpose in my life.

Everlasting Father

'And he will be called . . . Everlasting Father' (v. 6).

We usually associate the name of Father with the first Person of the Godhead, but here the title belongs to Christ. However, the original text does not denote 'father' in the usual association we have with that word. It means in this verse author or possessor. A more exact rendering of this verse would be 'the Father of Eternity' as it is rendered by the *Amplified Bible*. Thus, this verse speaks of Christ as the Eternal One and as the One who holds eternity in his possession. Vast, unfathomable eternity is his.

One of the most intriguing exercises for the imagination is to consider the eternity of Jesus. It staggers the mind. Jesus always was; he had no beginning. As God, he is the great First Cause of all things. If we could turn back time and look down the dim corridor of the ages we would find Jesus with the Father at the beginning. He was there when the plants and universe were created. He is the Unbeginning One.

People ask, 'Who *were* Buddha and Napoleon?' But always, 'Who *is* Jesus Christ?' Not only is Jesus Lord of the past and the present, but as the possessor of eternity he holds the future in his hands. Jesus the timeless holds all time in his hands. We may not know what the future holds, but we know who holds the future.

In one of those texts that stands as a sovereign mountain peak of truth that dominates the landscape of life, we read: 'He has also set eternity in the hearts of men' (Ecclesiastes 3:11). All around us God has put intimations of our immortality. There is within us an unrelenting intuition to see beyond temporal horizons and to press beyond the limits of the finite. Eternal forces ripple in our blood.

Paul affirms: 'The gift of God is eternal life in Christ Jesus our Lord' (Romans 6:23). What a soul-stirring truth – Jesus Christ shares his eternity with us! Because Jesus Christ is eternal and he has made us joint heirs with him, we shall share eternity with him.

Stories That Are Seen

The series of readings and comments for Sundays is collated from Stories That
Are Seen *and* More Stories That Are Seen, *two sets of studies on the parables
of Jesus written by Lieutenant-Colonel Douglas Clarke. These books, published
by The Salvation Army's Australia Eastern Territory in 2002 and 2008, aim to
help readers become amazed again by the truth and personal impact of Jesus'
familiar and best-loved stories.*

Introduction

Why study the parables? What relevance do these stories, told in first-
century rural Palestine, have for the twenty-first century? Has the
sheer power of the originality, freshness and impact of these stories been
lost in preaching and translation? To the contrary! The parables of Jesus
need to be rediscovered and applied to our Christian discipleship and
spirituality, and to today's Church and society.

No part of the Gospels accounts of the life and ministry of Jesus brings
us more directly into contact with his mind, than these stories. The
fifteenth-century monk, Thomas à Kempis, commenced his classic
The Imitation of Christ with these words: 'Let the life of Jesus Christ, then,
be our first consideration. The teaching of Jesus far transcends all the
teachings of the saints, and whosoever has his Spirit will discover
concealed in it heavenly manna.'

Such is the importance of the Lord's teaching that we find in the first
three Gospels more than sixty parables – some of one or two verses, many
of considerable length – all with the main theme 'The kingdom of God'. In
studying the parables we can be sure that we are in direct contact with the
mind of Jesus of Nazareth.

Be a Neighbour

'He asked Jesus, "And who is my neighbour?"' (v. 29).

The parable of the good Samaritan, taught by Jesus, is a commentary on the Old Testament command to 'love your neighbour as yourself' (Leviticus 19:18). It is given in response to the question posed by a theologian of the law of Moses, about the meaning of 'neighbour'.

In this period of his life and ministry, in his final weeks before the crucifixion, Jesus is travelling with his disciples towards Jerusalem, accompanied by the crowds. On the journey Jesus is approached by one of the experts in the law who was intent on testing Jesus' knowledge of the sacred law. 'Teacher, what must I do to inherit eternal life?' he asks (v. 25). Jesus responds with counter questions, which direct the theologian to the Old Testament: 'What is written in the Law? . . . How do you read it?' (v. 26).

Suddenly, it is the lawyer's understanding of the Old Testament law which is being tested by Jesus. The lawyer replies by quoting Deuteronomy 6:5 and Leviticus 19:18, the command regarded as forming the very heart and soul of the Jewish religion. Jesus responds by accepting the lawyer's answer: 'You have answered correctly . . . do this and you will live' (Luke 10:28).

The lawyer has the correct theology but the question remains – is the lawyer willing to act on it? Aware that he has lost the initiative to Jesus, the lawyer, still convinced that he can emerge from this encounter fully justified, puts a further question to Jesus: 'And who is my neighbour?' (v. 29).

Jesus responds by not answering the lawyer's further question directly, but instead tells the memorable story of the caring Samaritan. Jesus told the story not to answer the lawyer's question but to show him that it was the wrong question to ask. The right question to ask is not 'Who is my neighbour?' but 'To whom can I be a neighbour?'! The answer is to anyone whose need claims my assistance and demands my availability.

How does this impact my Christian discipleship as I live in an increasingly multicultural, multi-religious and multiracial society?

Arm of the Lord

'To whom has the arm of the LORD been revealed?' (53:1).

Isaiah, in the chapter that speaks so eloquently of the sacrifice of Christ, exclaims: 'Who has believed our message and to whom has the arm of the LORD been revealed?' 'Arm' was a figure of speech for power, decisive action. Christ was the decisive action of the Eternal to bring deliverance and salvation, sublimely described in the remainder of this chapter.

The word 'revealed' indicates that he had been hidden. For centuries, the prophets and people of God had been standing on tiptoe, awaiting the promised Messiah. Then, in the event of the ages, in that miracle and marvel of the manger in Bethlehem, the arm of the Lord became revealed. That rough-hewn manger cradled the destiny of man and his hopes of all the years. It was the moment of God's supreme revelation.

The Emperor Constantine built a church over the cave believed to have been the birthplace of Christ. As you descend into that cave of the nativity, now under the high altar of the church, the opening is such that you must stoop or kneel to enter. In the floor is a Latin inscription: 'Here Jesus Christ was born of the Virgin Mary.'

There is something beautifully symbolic in the fact that the pilgrim has to kneel to enter the birthplace of our Lord, for to contemplate his birth fills the soul with awe and reverence. We kneel before the miracle of the God of creation, revealing his love in a babe!

But the arm of the Lord was further revealed – in his magnificent life, his suffering and death, the triumph of his resurrection and ascension. Still he is being revealed to his followers by the Holy Spirit. And, some day, he will reveal himself again in his mighty return.

Who has believed the message? To whom is the arm of the Lord revealed? Just think – to you and me!

Prayer

Heavenly Father, thank you for the love that brought Christ to earth and went all the way to Calvary for me.

Star

'A star will come out of Jacob' (Numbers 24:17).

The story of Balaam is one of the most puzzling portions in the Old Testament (Numbers 22:5–24:25). He feared God, but worshipped gold; a prophet of the Most High, but also a sorcerer who pronounced blessings on Israel, but told how it could be destroyed – a pitiful example of Christ's warning, we cannot serve God and mammon.

Balak, King of Moab, sent for Balaam, asking him to curse Israel. In the end, Balaam did so and calamity resulted. Balaam was slain and 24,000 Israelites perished (Numbers 25:9; 31:8, 16). Balaam's name became a byword for greed (Jude 11) and treachery (Revelation 2:14).

But before Balaam succumbed to greed and treachery, he pronounced four remarkable prophecies of the place Israel would have in history and God's blessing on them as a nation. His fourth prophecy contained an extraordinary vision: 'I see him, but not now; I behold him, but not near. A star will come out of Jacob'.

Man knows of nothing in the physical world that can compare to the glow and grandeur of the stars. Their colossal size and incomputable energy are mind-boggling to consider. Their unerring precision has enabled man to chart his way through pathless seas.

To the Christian, Christ is our star, the unerring guide leading us safely through our journey of life. In the universe of the spirit, the grandeur and glory of Jesus Christ is without comparison.

With Horatius Bonar, Christians can sing:

> I heard the voice of Jesus say: I am this dark world's light;
> Look unto me, thy morn shall rise and all thy day be bright.
> I looked to Jesus, and I found in him my star, my sun;
> And in that light of life I'll walk till travelling days are done.
>
> *(SASB* 332, v. 3)

Prayer

Christ, be the star of my life that I may know your radiance, your power, your guidance.

Wonderful Counsellor

'And he will be called Wonderful Counsellor' (Isaiah 9:6).

Life is often perplexing, bewildering, complex, problematic, disconcerting. We have an inescapable need for the Divine Counsellor who advises, instructs and guides. He is involved in the intimacies of life, directing us through its crises. It is a staggering, sacred responsibility.

A counsellor needs to be close, accessible. Christ is as close as the whisper of a prayer, always available, never away or too busy. The confidential aspect of *counselling* is inherent in Christ's counselling to his followers. To him, we can take the most intimate matters of the heart. To him we are not a case, but a child; not a problem person, but a person with a problem and potential. He knows our needs and he knows what is best for us.

Some counsellors fail because they never achieve a thorough understanding of the person. It is difficult indeed to penetrate the subtleties of human emotions, motivation and the make-up of our subconscious, which dictates so much of our conscious life. As John says of Jesus: 'He knew all men. He did not need man's testimony about man, for he knew what was in a man' (2:24–25). Jesus Christ knows and understands us better than we know ourselves.

We can communicate to Christ in prayer. And prayer is a dialogue rather than a monologue. If we exercise the discipline of silence and stillness, Christ speaks to us through inward promptings, the engenderings of conviction, the sensitising of conscience, the gentle stirrings of his Spirit. And he has left for us his counsellor's manual for the human heart in the communication of his word.

We may with confidence bring to him the hurts, failures, deep needs and aspirations of our lives. For Christ is the counsellor par excellence. He is the Wonderful Counsellor.

Prayer

Wonderful Counsellor, I would yield my foolishness to your wisdom, my perplexity to your guidance, my darkness to your light, my future to your prescience, my life to your way and will.

9

Prince of Peace

'And he will be called . . . Prince of Peace' (v. 6).

The world cries out for peace. The devoted effort of so many world leaders and diplomats is on behalf of peace. Yet history seems to confirm the futility of man's search for peace. A historian estimated that over 3,000 years there had been thirteen years of war for every year of peace.

Today, nuclear destruction threatens; but this is not only the era of the split atom but of the split personality as well. Man is beset by neuroses and psychoses so many and varied that they have been charted all the way from A to Z: acrophobia, fear of heights, to zoophobia, fear of animals. The classic words of Henry Thoreau seem more apposite to our age than to his: 'The mass of men lead lives of quiet desperation.'

Peace is not so much an external climate as an inward experience. As Prince of Peace, Jesus imparts his peace in three primary ways:

First, he enables us to have peace *with God* by his work of reconciliation. The cross of Calvary was a great bridge across the impassable chasm of sin. It led the way from man's fallen condition back to his holy Creator.

Second, Jesus enables us to have peace *within ourselves*. He resolves the inner conflicts, cross purposes and tensions which act as bandits robbing us of serenity. He quells the civil war within the heart, between the carnal and the spiritual nature, by the power and work of the Holy Spirit.

When we are at peace with God and with ourselves, then we will be at peace in the third area of relationship – *with others*. When the vertical relationship is right then the horizontal relationship will take on its proper perspective.

The prophet Isaiah elsewhere gives us the secret of peace: 'You will keep in perfect peace him whose mind is steadfast, because he trusts in you' (26:3). When our hearts and minds are centred on Christ, we will know his serenity amid storms.

The Lord, Our Righteousness

'He will be called: The LORD Our Righteousness' (v. 6).

'Then they will go away to eternal punishment, but the righteous to eternal life' are the final words of the 'Olivet Discourse' of Christ dealing with the end of the age (Matthew 24:3–25:46). Our Lord makes quite clear that only the righteous will go to heaven and have eternal life. But that poses a problem. Isaiah confesses for all of us: 'All our righteous acts are like filthy rags' (64:6). And Paul reinforces this truth: 'There is no-one righteous, not even one' (Romans 3:10).

What then is the answer to our dilemma? With Paul we also may say: 'That I may gain Christ and be found in him, not having a righteousness of my own that comes from the law, but that which is through faith in Christ – the righteousness that comes from God and is by faith' (Philippians 3:8, 9). By the merit of the vicarious sacrifice of Christ for our sin, his righteousness is imputed to us.

A Greek legend tells of Theseus who volunteered to be locked in the vast labyrinth beneath the city of Minos. He faced two dangers underground: the minotaur who devoured all those he trapped within, and the maze itself, a vast network of intricate tunnels. But Ariadne secretly slipped him a spool of thread. By unravelling it as he pursued the minotaur, Theseus laid a trail to find his way back. Without the thread, he would have wandered, hopelessly lost.

As we seek to overcome Satan's destructive power, and make our way through earth's maze to that eternal city, the righteousness of Christ alone will enable us to attain that ultimate goal of our life.

Nicolaus Zinzendorf's hymn gives expression to this truth:

> Jesus, Thy blood and righteousness
> My beauty are, my glorious dress . . .
> (*SASB* 116)

Prayer

Lord, help me to hunger and thirst after righteousness.

11

Son of David

'The genealogy of Jesus Christ the Son of David' (Matthew 1:1).

This title may not seem significant to us today. However, the first question put forward in Christ's day about an alleged Messiah would be, 'Is he of the house of David?' Every devout Jew knew God had promised, through his prophets, that the Messiah would come from King David's line.

Matthew has arranged his genealogy into three divisions of fourteen generations each. The first period takes us from Abraham to David, from patriarchs and judges to the period of the monarchy. The second, from David to the Exile, represents both the flowering and the fading of the kingdom.

The final period of Exile, and after, was a time when Israel could have passed into oblivion except for divine providence. But all through these critical periods, God preserved the line of David from which would come Christ. History is his story.

In the genealogy are four remarkable women: Tamar; and Rahab; the righteous but non-Jewish Ruth; and 'Uriah's wife', mother of Solomon. Some other names represent anything but luminaries on the horizon of history. The last ten names are unrecorded in the Old Testament, but how wonderfully God used the weak things, the seemingly insignificant, to bring about his purpose! Each one of the names listed was a vital link in God's chain of history.

This title also links Jesus with humanity. He was born of earthly parentage. Though God, he became a man. He created worlds and companied with celestial beings, yet came to live in a family setting on earth.

Christ, a descendant of the royal line of David, transcended all the royalty that was represented in the title. He brought a glory and a grandeur to the throne of David that will be undimmed and undiminished throughout eternal ages. He who is the Son of God became the Son of David, that we might be of his *spiritual* lineage and be forever adopted sons of God.

Return of the Prodigal

'His father saw him, and his heart went out to him. He ran to meet him,
flung his arms round him, and kissed him' (v. 20, NEB).

In Sir John Soane's Museum, Lincoln's Inn Field, London, is a series of eight paintings, titled 'A Rake's Progress', by the eighteenth-century English artist, William Hogarth. In this moving series of paintings Hogarth depicts the journey of Tom Rakewell's prodigal lifestyle and subsequent demise. The second of the eight paintings shows young Tom Rakewell entering London to spend his father's wealth recklessly. The eighth and final painting in the series shows Tom totally humiliated, naked and insane.

What a contrast to the conclusion of our Lord's story, where, unlike Hogarth's prodigal, the prodigal coming to his senses returns home and is accepted by a loving and forgiving father.

In first-century Palestine a son would not normally receive his inheritance until the death of his father. In his study of the parables Kenneth Bailey observes that in all Middle Eastern literature, aside from this parable, from ancient times to the present, there is no case of any son, older or younger, asking for his inheritance from a father who is still in good health. Such a request represents an extraordinary insult and behaviour that was totally unacceptable. In effect the lad was saying, 'Dad, I wish you were dead!'

Following the squandering of the inheritance in riotous living, the lad found himself in a desperate situation. So desperate that he, a Jew, was reduced to looking after pigs – animals seen to be unclean and owned by a Gentile! And even worse: sharing the pigs' feeding trough for carob-bean pods. There is an old rabbinical saying which states that when the Israelites are reduced to eating carob-pods then they repent.

Certainly for this young man, he had reached the point of desperation. It is at this point in his personal journey that he came to his senses (v. 17). So he set out for his father's house.

Repentance is not an act of human humility or human self-mastery. To the contrary, it is being overwhelmed by the grace and mercy of God our Father.

13

Redeemer

*'I know that my Redeemer lives, and that in the end he will
stand upon the earth' (v. 25).*

From Job, the Shakespeare of the Old Testament, we have a textual jewel,
shining all the brighter because of its night-enshrouded setting. Job had
experienced the loss of his possessions, children and health; the reproof of
his wife, and the suspicion of his friends. Yet still he proclaims: 'I know that
my Redeemer lives.'

The Hebrew word he uses, *goel*, represented the kinsman whose duty it
was to recover a captured or enslaved relative. We were captives of sin and
Satan. Jesus delivered us from this enslavement and made us free. The
concept *goel* also required the kinsman to recover sold or forfeited
inheritance. The loss of paradise was for man a tragedy. Sin made him
forfeit his spiritual inheritance. But Christ, our redeemer, has recovered
our lost estate for us if we will accept his act of redemption. He is our great
kinsman, winning back for us that which we had lost.

This text is animated with three vital concepts – immortality,
resurrection, and the return of Jesus Christ. It proclaims a message most
needed in the world today – Christ is alive and will some day re-enter our
troubled and tortured world. In the grand dénouement of creation, 'he will
stand upon the earth'.

Job, through his telescope of faith, perceived this towering truth of the
Old Testament. In one of the rare references before Christ to immortality,
he exclaimed: 'After my skin has been destroyed, yet in my flesh I will see
God' (v. 26). This statement is a landmark of faith and truth in the Old
Testament. Mankind had to await the resurrection of our Lord and the
insights of the New Testament before immortality came into clear focus
for the believer.

_____

Prayer

**Jesus, my kinsman, thank you for redeeming my soul from the clutches of Satan
and for pardon gained through your grace.**

The Word

'His name is the Word of God' (v. 13).

The Greeks had three words for *word*. One meant the sound of a voice, another was a sound revealing a mental state and the third was *logos*, the 'Word' of our text. One of the great words of the Greek New Testament, *logos* combines the thoughts of expression and wisdom. Not being easily translatable into English, Moffatt leaves *logos* untranslated and renders John 1:1 (*JMT*) as:

> The Logos existed in the very beginning,
> the Logos was with God,
> the Logos was divine.

Philo, a first-century Alexandrian Jew, fused the Greek and Jewish thought on the word *logos* and, through his writings, this word gained significant currency, communicating effectively to both Jew and Greek. But Christ was bigger even than this great word and filled it with new meaning.

As the Word, Christ was God become *vocal*. No longer would human prophets give a gradual unfolding of the divine message. God would speak his great and glorious message through his Son. Christ became the ultimate medium of communication from God to man. Through Christ, God speaks to man in a new and living language – the language of life in Christ Jesus.

Our text in Revelation speaks of the Word as having his robe dipped in blood. We are reminded that he spoke God's message most eloquently in his sacrifice and death. The cross was the 'bulletin board' on which God proclaimed to the world his amnesty for rebellious sinners.

As the Word, Christ was God become *visible*. Although centuries separate us from Milton and Shakespeare, their words reveal their thoughts and philosophies. But, as the Word of God, Christ portrays the mind and heart of God. He unveils the mysterious, mighty, magnificent and majestic God. He brings the God of the universe into the heart of man upon earth.

Jesus

*'You are to give him the name Jesus, because he will save
his people from their sins' (v. 21).*

Our verse starts with a declaration: 'You are to give'. The name Jesus
was the name God himself chose. It is the name by which we know
him best. It is his 'earthly' name. Other names and titles were ascribed to
him in special ways and for a specific purpose, but this is his primary
name. In the Gospels, it occurs 500 times, and a total of 909 times in the
New Testament.

Of all the names and titles of Christ this has been most endearing to his
followers. Well-known hymns add eloquent testimony of that fact. John
Newton gave us, 'How sweet the name of Jesus sounds'; Edward Perronet
exalts this name with, 'All hail the power of Jesus' name!'; Lydia Baxter
earnestly enjoins, 'Take the name of Jesus with you'; Frederick Whitfield
exclaims, 'There is a name I love to hear.'

Jesus is the name that denotes the great purpose of his life. Above all else
he came to be our Saviour! The names Jesus and Joshua are the same.
Joshua is the Hebrew equivalent of the Greek Jesus. Many Bible scholars
consider Joshua to have been a prototype of Christ. Joshua led the Israelites
from the wilderness to the Promised Land. Jesus as Saviour brings us from
the wilderness of sin into our spiritual Promised Land. Joshua led his
people to conquests over their enemies with their walled cities. Jesus leads
us to conquest over the enemies of our soul.

He enables us to fight victoriously against life's difficult obstacles and its
giants of temptation, trial and testing. As our Joshua, he leads us to the
inheritance God has for us – a land spiritually 'flowing with milk and
honey'.

Jesus, of course, far transcended Joshua's work of salvation among the
people. Joshua's deliverance foreshadowed and prefigured the One who
would give ultimate fulfilment to this great name. The Scriptures declare:
'Salvation is found in no-one else, for there is no other name under heaven
given to men by which we must be saved' (Acts 4:12).

Immanuel

'The virgin will be with child and will give birth to a son, and they will call him Immanuel – which means, "God with us"' (v. 23).

Immanuel is written just three times in God's Word. In the Gospel account, the angel is quoting the prophet Isaiah. Christ alone was great enough to be called Immanuel. No one else could be called 'God with us'. John writes that he 'became flesh (human, incarnate), and tabernacled – fixed His tent of flesh, lived awhile – among us; and we [actually] saw His glory' (John 1:14, *AB*). This thought is a stupendous one. It staggers the imagination. Yet that is precisely what happened with the incarnation.

The miracle and the marvel of Immanuel – God with us – defies description. Jesus was the heart of God wrapped in human flesh. He was God in the garb of humanity. He was God walking the earth in sandals. For the first time on planet Earth, the voice of God was heard from human vocal chords. Immanuel speaks to us of the mighty miracle and marvel of God becoming man and dwelling with us.

A young child looked at a picture of her absent father and said, 'I wish Father would step out of that picture.' For centuries, men had a yearning for God to step out of the picture – to become more real, more tangible to man. At Bethlehem, God became flesh – became real, understandable to men. Jesus was God's authentic self-disclosure.

What a reassuring thought it is that he is still Immanuel to his followers! He is still God with us. He has promised, 'Surely I am with you always, to the very end of the age' (Matthew 28:20). We follow the One who said, 'Never will I leave you; never will I forsake you' (Hebrews 13:5).

He is always the contemporary Christ. He is superior to all life's vicissitudes, surviving death itself. He will walk with us through its valley into the house of the Lord, where we shall dwell with him for ever.

Brother

*'Isn't this Mary's son and the brother of James, Joseph, Judas and Simon?
Aren't his sisters here with us?' (Mark 6:3).*

At least six siblings knew Jesus as brother. Jesus no doubt often played the elder brother's part. James, Joseph, Judas, Simon and the sisters would often be helped by Jesus, who was a loving and faithful older brother. But one verse in the Gospels invests this title with deep spiritual meaning. We read: 'Whoever does the will of my Father in heaven is my brother' (v. 50). To every believer, Jesus is the Elder Brother.

A truck driver was once caught in a roaring blizzard. Driving became impossible. He pulled the big truck off the road and went to sleep. When he awoke, everything was dark. Buried in a snowdrift thirty feet deep, no part of his truck was visible from the highway. He could not open the doors. He was trapped. For five days and nights he stayed in his icy tomb. But he didn't panic. He waited, calmly and stoically, to be rescued; and finally he was.

When asked if he was afraid, he answered, 'No. I knew my brother would be looking for me. I knew he would not rest until he found me. In my mind I could see him searching, searching, never giving up.' The story powerfully illustrates the text from Proverbs: 'A brother is born for adversity' (17:17).

How blessed is one who has such a brother; by blood, or by spiritual bond! The friendship of Jesus is the highest privilege and greatest blessing of life. As Henry van Dyke has written:

> Thou the Father, Christ, our brother –
> All who live in love are thine;
> Teach us how to love each other,
> Lift us to the joy divine.
>
> (*SASB* 10)

Prayer

Thank you, Lord, for this special relationship we are privileged to have with you as our brother.

Prophet

'The crowds answered, "This is Jesus, the prophet from Nazareth in Galilee" ' (v. 11).

To the devout believer of biblical days, prophets were of the highest rank and order among men. When awed by Jesus' miracles or witnessing a demonstration of his deep wisdom or great power, people often acclaimed him a prophet. It was the highest compliment that could be given to a man. Specially chosen and anointed by God, the prophet was God's mouth-piece.

Each Old Testament prophet gave some new insight concerning God. Isaiah's sublime passages reveal God's holiness and give incomparable predictions of the coming Messiah; Jeremiah reveals the significance of personal religion; Ezekiel depicts God's special relationship with Israel; through Hosea, God bares his heart of forgiveness for the backslider; Amos thunders God's declarations for the application of religion to the ills of society.

Each prophet, out of his own life and experience, expressed a fragment, a facet of truth about God. But Jesus, as prophet, reveals the full truth about God. He is himself a revelation of what God is like. He is the embodiment of divine attributes. He alone could say, 'He who has seen me has seen the Father.' He is the Prophet who gives, not a fragmentary knowledge, but a full disclosure of God.

Jesus supremely fulfils the office of a prophet. But Jesus was more than a prophet. He was the fulfilment of the prophecies that had gone before. Other prophets had been called and commissioned to prepare the way for him. He was the Sun of Righteousness towards which all their flickering torches pointed.

Viewing Christ as a prophet is a window through which we gain a greater and grander view of his nature and mission. Compared to his brightness and glory, all other prophets were as flashing meteorites which appeared briefly on the horizon and quickly burned themselves out. He transcends the prophets and fulfils their God-given oracles.

Prayer

Pre-eminent Christ, rule and reign over all else in my heart and life.

Family Feud

*'The older brother stalked off in an angry sulk and refused to
join in. His father came out and tried to talk to him,
but he wouldn't listen' (vv. 28, 29, MSG).*

With the return home of the younger son, Jesus turns to the elder whilst maintaining, as he did in the first part of the story, the focus upon the waiting, compassionate father. The elder brother's attitudes and sullen spirit locked him out of what should have been a time of joy, forgiveness and reconciliation. On hearing the sound of music and dancing, and learning that the father had killed the fatted calf, he was angry and refused to go in.

In spite of Middle Eastern custom requiring the eldest son to present himself at the banquet – for he would be expected to move among the guests offering compliments – he chose to humiliate his father publicly, by sulking and refusing to join in with the celebrations.

Over many years there had grown in the elder brother's spirit a deep, smouldering hatred for his father. The return of the younger son coupled with the father's response fanned the smouldering hatred into an all-consuming flame of bitterness and anger.

Will the older son be prepared to kneel and acknowledge that all he has comes to him because of his father's love? And for my part, am I prepared to kneel – or do I want a pat on the head because of my faithful service?

Some of the big questions we will have to answer merge out of this story: Has the joy of working for my Father turned to drudgery? Do I feel I am superior in God's sight because I have worked faithfully for many years? Am I organised to accumulate or to receive?

Yes! It may be counter to my pride, my dignity, but this story teaches that in brokenness and total helplessness, with no merit of our own, our loving Father pours out his astonishing love, mercy and grace.

To Be Like Jesus

This series is collated from chapters of Holiness Unwrapped, *by Commissioner Robert Street. The book, published by The Salvation Army's Australia Eastern Territory in 2005, has its focus on Jesus as both the example and spiritual source for holy living.*

Introduction

There's no better aim for a Christian than to be like Jesus – and there's no better way to become more like him than to let him live his life in us. Jesus exemplifies everything we could hope to be and what we ought to be. His goodness shines like a beacon in a world darkened by wrongdoing and self-interest.

So it's no surprise that in our complex postmodern era, which often has no clear-cut solutions, many Christians find themselves frequently asking the question, 'What would Jesus do?' Faced with challenging or difficult situations, people the world over look to Jesus for guidance and direction – wanting their actions to reflect him.

Significantly, he left in the Gospels guidelines for daily living and lived by them himself. He proved their worth and set us an example. He showed by his own life that what he taught could be successfully embraced.

In Old Testament times, the holy God could seem distant and remote – to be so far above us that he was in 'splendid isolation'. Then Jesus came. He literally brought God down to earth. And he showed us, in human form, what a holy life was really like. Jesus was holiness unwrapped. As we see in him what we would like to be, he is more than willing to help us.

Holy

'For them I sanctify myself, that they too may be truly sanctified' (v. 19).

When we think of Jesus we think of someone who is holy – supremely holy. When we look at ourselves we see imperfections, flaws in our character, and disappointments. There is a gap that needs bridging. Jesus came to earth to bridge that gap – and to make it possible for us to live holy lives. He prayed for our sanctification (vv. 17–23), and so indicated it was possible.

The word 'holy' finds its roots in the Greek New Testament word *hagios* or *hagiasmos*. It speaks of the separateness of God – a strong Old Testament concept. The almighty, everlasting and all-seeing God was acknowledged as being far above his creation in every sense (Psalm 8). He was uncontaminated, pure, separate – holy.

When Jesus came to live among us as God's Son, he brought his holiness with him. He was God Incarnate – fully human (Philippians 2:7). He was bridging the gap just by being here. More than that, he showed by his own actions what a holy life looked like. He taught how it could be lived. He promised the help we need to live it (John 14:26).

Jesus didn't demonstrate his holiness by wearing a halo round his head, or by keeping a safe distance from people who might contaminate him with their ways or ideas. He demonstrated it by being 'tempted in every way, just as we are – yet [being] without sin' (Hebrews 4:15). He remained undefiled, even though he was totally involved in the lives of those around him.

His holiness showed itself in a sinless life, by his purity of motive, by the evidence of grace and truth in all his dealings. He was humble, compassionate, forgiving and obedient to God the Father, from whom he sought constant guidance and strength.

As we consider these characteristics of Jesus, we will remind ourselves not only that he calls us to keep our sinful nature under control, but also to live positively to his glory among our friends and neighbours – and even our enemies! (Matthew 5:44).

Vulnerable

'For when I am weak, then I am strong' (v. 10).

To have a newborn baby placed in your arms and to be responsible for looking after this young life can't help but remind any of us of the vulnerability of the baby. He or she is so helpless – totally dependent. Imagine how Mary and Joseph felt when Jesus – the Saviour of the world – was born into their care. Imagine, too, just how vulnerable God made himself by coming in Jesus to earth.

Jesus' vulnerability was evident from the start. Herod tried to have him killed and Mary and Joseph fled to Egypt to escape the slaughter (Matthew 2:16, 19–21). When Jesus began his ministry there were others waiting to exploit his vulnerability. His teaching outraged the religious people and the rulers. He refused to be drawn into political power games and spoke God's message – unequivocally, sometimes tenderly, but always truly.

In the end, his vulnerability was cruelly exploited as he was arrested on trumped-up charges, falsely accused, wrongly condemned, mocked, beaten, whipped and humiliated. Eventually he was murdered – on a cross. He hung there helplessly – as helpless as a babe it seemed, especially when he cried out, 'My God, my God, why have you forsaken me?' (Matthew 27:46).

The mystery is that the One hanging on the cross was still God Almighty being true to himself. We – the accusers and murderers – were (and are) the helpless ones. We needed him more than anything else in the world. He alone could save us from ourselves and from our sins. His 'helplessness' was our salvation.

Some of us find it easier than others to make ourselves vulnerable – to be open, to meet people halfway, to share what belongs to us. Others find it very difficult. In Christ we see someone who encourages us to dare to make ourselves vulnerable so that we can meet people at their point of need. And he promises his strength to make up for our weakness (2 Corinthians 12:9).

A People Person

'For the Son of Man came to seek and to save what was lost' (v. 10).

It's difficult to read the Gospels without realising that Jesus was a people person. There were times when people frustrated him (Mark 8:18) and when he simply needed to get away from them (Mark 1:35), but his commitment to people is unquestionable.

Zacchaeus was waiting for someone to believe in him (Luke 19:1–10). He was a disreputable man. Working for the Roman occupiers as a tax collector, he lived by cheating his fellow countrymen. When Jesus stopped to talk to him and invited himself to stay in his home, the transformation in Zacchaeus was remarkable. Zacchaeus believed in Jesus, but Jesus believed in him too – and in what he could become.

Jesus took time to talk to Mary (Luke 10:38–42). He talked to her about the things of God and she drank up every word. Nicodemus, one of the Jewish ruling council, came to Jesus by night. He shared with him some of his most important teachings (John 3:1–21).

Time and again Jesus took individuals out of the crowd to talk with them and heal them. He spoke to a disreputable woman at a well in Samaria (John 4:1–30) and rescued an adulteress from her self-righteous accusers (John 8:1–11).

Even so, people frequently let him down – including those closest to him. The disciples often misunderstood him, made a priority of their own importance and even failed him in the Garden of Gethsemane when he specifically asked them to pray with him at such a crucial time (Matthew 26:36–41). But he coped with their unpredictability and failures – and he also deals with ours today.

We will often be frustrated, disappointed, disillusioned and sometimes wonder why we bother. People make promises they don't keep, take each other for granted and can sometimes be very dislikeable. Jesus never gave up on people – even those who let him down the most. As we try to follow his example, his confidence that others can be transformed encourages us to believe so too.

A Servant

'Your attitude should be the same as that of Christ Jesus' (v. 5).

The supreme and guiding example of service comes from Jesus. The concept of God serving his own creation is beyond the comprehension of other religions, but not Christianity.

Writing to the Philippians, the apostle Paul drew attention to a standard for Christians of all generations: 'Your attitude should be the same as that of Christ Jesus: Who, being in very nature God . . . made himself nothing, taking the very nature of a servant, being made in human likeness' (vv. 5–7).

When Jesus announced his own mission (Luke 4:16–21) he used words from Isaiah 61:1, 2 which portrayed him as the Servant of Jehovah: 'The Spirit of the Lord is on me, because he has anointed me to preach good news to the poor. He has sent me to proclaim freedom for the prisoners and recovery of sight for the blind, to release the oppressed, to proclaim the year of the Lord's favour.'

The realities of life for Jesus – his serving us – included being subjected to the worst of human behaviour, leading eventually to his horrific murder. For Jesus, servanthood – service to mankind – was not about running around doing good deeds. It was doing for us what we could not do for ourselves. It was doing what needed to be done. It cost him dearly.

He still serves us, showing the true heart of God. Significantly, his authority seems heightened by his servanthood, not diminished. He is seen to be authentic. When he asks us to serve he is not asking anything he wasn't or isn't prepared to do himself. The implications for us are clear. If we are to follow Jesus – to become like him – we must embrace servanthood too. In effect, the only authority he gives us is to serve.

Jesus served by doing what his Father had instructed, by being obedient to his will (Philippians 2:8). So should we. Jesus' washing of the disciples' feet was not only a symbolic act. It expressed the true heart of God (John 13:1–17). 'No servant is greater than his master' (v. 16), he said. If Jesus kneels to serve, so should we.

Passionate

'As he approached Jerusalem and saw the city, he wept over it' (v. 41).

Any initial consideration of instances where Jesus showed passion would probably include the turning over of the tables in the temple where, said Jesus, the money-changers had turned God's house into a den of robbers (v. 46). Jesus was obviously incensed at the abuse and misuse of this sacred place.

He also showed great passion when speaking of the abuse suffered by children at the hands of adults. It would be better for such a person, said Jesus, 'to have a large millstone hung around his neck and to be drowned in the depths of the sea' (Matthew 18:6). Jesus also had strong words for the Pharisees, and Matthew 23 explains why he saw them as hypocrites.

But Jesus' passion was shown in other ways too. He wept over Jerusalem and at the sorrow caused by the death of Lazarus (John 11:35). The Gospels record him being moved with compassion for individuals with specific needs and for crowds of people. He gave of himself time and time again, spending his energy and love on them. Most of all, he was so passionate about his people that he died for them. It is not by accident that the last hours of Jesus are known as the Passion and that the true meaning of 'passion' is suffering.

We shouldn't assume that passion of itself is a virtue. It can be used to good effect and to bad. Passion gets things achieved, mountains conquered and relief programmes put in place. It also destroys, distorts and debases. When passion is mentioned in Scripture it is nearly always in the context of being dangerous (e.g. Galatians 5:24; Titus 2:2; 1 Peter 2:11).

The passion needed for a holy life is the passion which was in Christ – the passion to do his Father's will whatever the personal cost and however that should be expressed. Put simply, the holy life hands over its passions – all of them – to Jesus, so they can be centred in him, controlled by him, released by him.

Without Sin

*'We have one who has been tempted in every way, just as we are
– yet was without sin' (Hebrews 4:15).*

We know from human nature that we have a natural inclination to do what we ought not to do. We see children struggling with their behaviour from an early age. We read of Adam and Eve's curiosity and disobedience. We see it in ourselves at every age. The Bible calls these wilful actions 'sin' (Romans 3:9, 10). Today we usually refer to them as wrongdoing. What we call them doesn't matter so much as being prepared to admit we each have this inclination, and that we need to do something about it.

The apostle Paul bemoaned his own shortcomings: 'For what I do is not the good I want to do; no, the evil I do not want to do – this I keep doing' (Romans 7:19). Our behaviour tells us we are not without sin. In contrast, Jesus was without sin (Hebrews 4:15). He was tempted, but didn't give in. When he was baptised in the Jordan River by John the Baptist, it was not to rid himself of sin. It was to demonstrate to the world that he was completely surrendered to his Father's will.

The affirmation he received from God the Father was unequivocal: 'You are my Son, whom I love; with you I am well pleased' (Luke 3:22). By this Jesus was acknowledged as holy, set apart for God's will, but his next steps took him to the wilderness – to face temptation. We are told he conquered temptation being 'full of the Holy Spirit' (Luke 4:1). Having been tempted he understands our needs from experience and, by the same Holy Spirit, can give us the strength to resist temptation, controlling our sinful tendencies.

Sin weakens us. Our wrongdoing brings us shame. We may not always admit it – or even realise it – but it inevitably makes us less than we ought to be and has a negative effect on us and others. Paul knew this and asked, 'Who will rescue me?' (Romans 7:24). His answer was Jesus (v. 25).

We do not have to sin. We have the means whereby we can choose not to sin and call on Jesus to help us win the battle.

Dig Deep

*'What then of the man who hears these words of mine
and acts upon them?' (v. 24, NEB).*

This parable concludes Jesus' Sermon on the Mount as recorded in both Matthew's and Luke's Gospels. The appropriate title would be the parable of two builders, for it has as its focus the contrast between the wise builder who took care to build his house on rock deeply hidden below the surface and an unwise builder who recklessly built his house on sandy soil.

The story Jesus told would be true of the climatic conditions and terrain in Palestine. In Matthew's account of the parable, the imagery is of torrential autumn rains accompanied by a storm, which tested the building and its foundation. This is the type of picture Jesus is using as he speaks of the coming day of God's judgment.

In contrast to Matthew's account of the parable with its emphasis upon the impact of the storms, Luke's emphasis is upon the preparation of the foundations. John Calvin noted that 'true piety is not fully distinguished from its counterfeit till it comes to the time of testing'. Both Matthew and Luke record the storms as being a time of great crisis, of testing of the foundations of the houses.

We need to remember that this parable is teaching given to Christian disciples. Bible scholar John Stott comments that in this parable Jesus is not contrasting professing Christians with non-Christians who make no profession. On the contrary, what is common to both spiritual house-builders is that they 'hear these words of mine'. So both are members of the visible Christian community. Stott says the reason we often cannot tell the difference between them is that the foundations of their lives are hidden from view.

The question is not whether they *hear* Christ's teaching but whether they *do* what they hear. Am I content merely to be a nominal Christian paying lip service to Jesus and his teachings, or am I resolved to commit my whole life to Jesus and his mission?

Pure in Heart

'Create in me a pure heart, O God' (Psalm 51:10).

Choosing not to sin and finding strength to avoid wrongdoing are significant steps to becoming the person God intends us to be. Asking him to purify our hearts takes things further. It isn't only about not doing what should be avoided; it is about allowing God to make us what we should be. It is about who we are and what kind of person we are becoming.

Jesus' purity of heart showed itself in his selflessness. His motives were unselfish. He gave himself totally – to us and for us – in every good way, because he knew we needed him. When he called others to 'die to self' (see Luke 9:23) and follow him, he already knew from his own self-denying what he was asking them to do. There is no pure heart in someone whose personal wants and appetites come first. Scheming for our own ends, or manipulating other people (or situations) to our advantage, are in painful contrast to the holy life.

Jesus promised in the Beatitudes that the pure in heart would see God (Matthew 5:8). But we cannot manufacture our own pure heart. We aren't capable of it. The cleansing must come from Jesus – the One who alone can do it. It is a work of grace and it can only take place in humble, repentant people.

So, essentially, Jesus was talking about people whose hearts are made clean by God. This is the Holy Spirit's work. When he is invited into our lives – when our spiritual birth takes place (John 3:3) – the refining fire of the Holy Spirit purifies. We are made new. A fresh start takes place. Our hearts are made fit to be indwelt by Christ himself and empowered for living the holy life (Ephesians 3:17). A heart cleansed by God involves a washing away of all that has been unholy and indicates motives becoming purified, desires being refined and an intention to live a life surrendered to God.

Ultimately, a cleansed, renewed heart is an undeserved gift. It comes from a gracious God to those honest and humble enough to want it. A purified heart is an indescribable blessing.

Full of Grace and Truth

'For the grace of God that brings salvation has appeared to all men'
(Titus 2:11).

General John Larsson described Jesus as 'The man perfectly filled with the Spirit'. His book of that title shows Jesus as the supreme example of the Spirit of God fully indwelling a human being. God was in Christ (2 Corinthians 5:19) – and it showed. No room was given for what was unholy. The will of God was the will of Christ. The power of Christ was the power of God.

When John introduces Jesus at the beginning of his Gospel he defines him as being 'full of grace and truth' (1:4). Grace and truth go together in Jesus in full measure. They balance each other, complement each other and together show the heart of God. They are the perfect combination.

Truth indicates honesty, openness, nothing hidden. It has always been possible to distort, exaggerate, twist, deny, half-tell, ignore or reject the truth. But in Jesus – who called himself the Truth (John 14:6) – truth is personified. Also introduced by John as the Word (1:1), Jesus speaks transparently to the world without any falsehood. While on earth he represented the Father with supreme authenticity (15:15) and the words he spoke had eternal quality. As the Truth, Jesus presented the one and only standard by which we should measure our own living.

The truth is, of course, that not one of us has lived without sin. We have 'fallen short' of the glory of God (Romans 3:23) and it shows. The truth condemns us. As we have discovered, it is no use trying to hide the fact, either from ourselves or from God. This is where grace steps in (Romans 3:24). Titus speaks of Jesus as 'the grace of God that brings salvation' (2:11).

Grace is defined well as the undeserved favour of God. It is God seeing our shortcomings, yet providing the means by which we can be forgiven. It is in embracing the truth about our needy condition that we find God's grace and the freedom to be ourselves.

Truth and grace go together in the holy life.

A Man of Prayer

'Not my will, but yours be done' (Luke 22:42).

Jesus was a man of prayer. The Gospels show that he constantly kept in touch with God the Father by taking time to pray. He prayed when he was alone (Mark 1:35), withdrawing from the crowd (Luke 5:16). Sometimes he prayed all night (Luke 6:12). He drew strength from his relationship with his Father.

He prayed with his disciples (Luke 9:18). He prayed during deeply personal moments – such as his baptism (3:21) – and he prayed when he was engaged in day-to-day ministry (10:21). He prayed in his darkest moments – as at Gethsemane (22:41) and when he was dying (23:34).

Prayer was natural to Jesus. It can be natural to us.

Jesus was asked for guidance in prayer (Luke 11:1) and he gave it. He encouraged everyone to seek – and do – God's will, and to think of God as their heavenly Father (6:6). We can come to our Father with confidence, knowing he is ready to accept us (7:11). God even knows what we need before we ask, Jesus said (Matthew 6:8).

From this reassuring basis, Jesus spoke about what we should pray for and how we should pray. There's no need to babble on or to try to impress God (Matthew 6:6, 7). What we need most of all is to come quietly and humbly before God in open, honest relationship. Time set aside to be with God is invaluable, and prayer can take place anywhere at any time.

And the beauty of it is, we don't need to pretend to be different or better than we are. Prayer gives us opportunity to tell God what is on our hearts, and to let God tell us what we need to know and hear.

Jesus told us to pray for others – even those we find difficult (Matthew 5:44); to ask God for workers (9:38); to have faith when we pray (17:20).

Jesus also prayed for us – for our sanctification, our holiness (John 17:20) – so it was the prayer of God himself that we should be holy. Prayer is not an optional extra in holy living – and God asks us to join him in spirit and intercession as we pray for his world.

31

Consecrated

'For them I sanctify myself, that they too may be truly sanctified' (v. 19).

There were no half measures with Jesus. He not only came to be with and among us, he also came to give himself for us and to do so completely. He consecrated (sanctified) himself to the will of his Father and never deviated from it.

The old covenant (Testament) had proved impossible to keep. The law made its demands with the Ten Commandments at the centre but, as Jesus showed in the Sermon on the Mount, the spirit of the law was not being kept, let alone the letter of the law. Something new and better needed to happen. Jesus himself was the answer.

The fact is that Jesus came to do for us what we could not do for ourselves. The old covenant was in tatters because its demands had not been met (Hebrews 8:13). The new covenant, promised in Jeremiah 31:32, 33, wouldn't abolish the need for obedience, but by 'writing his laws on human hearts', God would give us his presence to help meet the covenant's demands.

It's no exaggeration to say that Jesus wrote the new covenant with his own blood. By doing so, he found his way into our hearts by love – an act which is as unequalled as it is unfathomable. The new covenant was costing him everything (Luke 22:20).

We make promises every day. Sometimes we make them legally. In church we make promises to God at various times and on specific occasions. We make promises in songs and hymns we sing and in prayers we speak on a regular basis. Sometimes we dare to make a covenant.

There are those who avoid making promises for fear of failing to keep them. Some make them and later regret it. Others find help from God to keep them. Jesus consecrated (sanctified) himself that his disciples might be truly sanctified (John 17:19). His prayer was for 'those who will believe in me through their message' (v. 20).

We have the privilege of responding to such a prayer by asking that God will work his work of grace in us – and consecrate us to his service.

Fruit of the Spirit

This series is adapted from a chapter in Never the Same Again, *by Retired General Shaw Clifton. Published in 1997 by Crest Books (The Salvation Army National Publications in the USA), the book is a helpful guide to the walk of faith for new Christians and others desiring to revisit the foundations of faith.*

Introduction

The phrase 'the fruit of the Spirit' from Galatians 5:22 can be used with the word 'fruit' or 'fruits'. In English, 'fruit' can be either singular or plural. The original Greek of the New Testament can be translated either way without damaging the meaning of the verse. There is no special doctrinal significance in saying either 'fruit' or 'fruits'. Notice that the *Good News Bible* avoids all this by saying simply 'the Spirit produces . . .'.

Let us consider each of the fruits in turn. Each is a way of being like Jesus. None is an optional extra. Every Christian should have all of the fruits in their life, to one extent or another. The more mature a Christian is, the more evident these things will be.

Try not to think of a bowl of fully ripe fruit, juicy and polished, begging to be picked up and eaten at the whim of the chooser. Think rather, when you ponder the fruit of the Spirit, of a small bud or tentative blossom that will slowly but steadily grow and grow into the fullness and maturity of the finished product.

Love

'Over all these virtues put on love' (v. 14).

Being loving comes first in the list in Galatians 5:22. This is not an accident. Love is the starting point from which all the other fruits grow. Take away love and all the fruits are strangled at birth. This love is not the sexual or romantic love felt between a man and a woman, or even the love which is shared in a family. It is the kind of love God has for you and me.

The Bible has a distinctive Greek word for it – *agape* (pronounced ag-a-pay). This is used every time the New Testament speaks of God's love for us. So it is a supernatural love which the Holy Spirit places within us. It goes on loving even if it is not returned, like God's love went on and on, even in the face of the rejection and crucifixion of Jesus.

The centrality of *agape* love in a Christian's life is spelled out for us in Colossians 3:12–14, where Paul speaks of compassion, kindness, humility, gentleness and patience, but goes on to single out love: 'And over all these virtues put on love (*agape*), which binds them all together in perfect unity.' This is why the great preacher, Dr W. E. Sangster, wrote that 'love is all the fruit in one'.

Pray then that the Holy Spirit will make you more loving: towards God, towards your fellow Christians and towards persons as yet unsaved. The practical consequences of this? No storing up grudges, no refusing to forgive, no moodiness, more acceptance of people as they are and a greater readiness to see what someone could become in Christ. How are you doing so far?

Joy

*'May you always be joyful in your union with the Lord.
I say it again: rejoice!' (v. 4, GNB).*

The New Testament is a book of joy. The verb 'to rejoice' and the noun 'joy' taken together crop up no less than 132 times! This joy is not some surface or temporary brightness of mood. Neither is it a general light-heartedness, or even a sense of optimism. Instead it is a deep-seated, inner state of ongoing, spiritual gladness, the seed of which is implanted in us by the Holy Spirit when we are saved.

Paul knows that such joy is a special mark of being a Christian, the hallmark of any person who is, like you, in union with the Lord. Try searching out the fifteen references to 'joy' or 'rejoice' in the letter to the Philippians and sense the extent to which the whole document is an epistle pulsating with joy! Two of the four Gospels begin and end with joy (see Matthew 2:10; 28:8 and Luke 2:10; 24:52) as if to signal that the joy we know as Christians is inextricably bound up with the coming of Jesus and with his life, death and resurrection.

You know for yourself the joy, the deep gladness of heart and soul, that floods over a person when they receive Christ as Saviour. The same joy is recorded in the New Testament when Zacchaeus welcomes the Lord (Luke 19:6); it is there again when Philip's preaching is well received in Samaria (Acts 8:8); and Paul is pleased to remind the believers in Thessalonica that when they first believed they 'welcomed the message with the joy given by the Holy Spirit' (1 Thessalonians 1:6).

One final point. Because the joy which is planted and nurtured in you by the Holy Spirit is a supernatural thing, no human being can rob you of it (see the words of Jesus in John 16:22). Your joy, therefore, can survive disappointments and frustrations, even circumstances of suffering or persecution, as did the joy of the Christians in Antioch despite efforts to suppress the gospel (Acts 13:52).

An Abundant Harvest (1)

The Sower and the Seed

*'He [Jesus] taught them many things by parables, and in his teaching said:
"Listen! A farmer went out to sow his seed"' (vv. 2, 3).*

Such is the importance of this parable that it is recorded in all three
synoptic Gospels. In Mark's Gospel this parable represents a significant turning point in Jesus' ministry in Galilee. The period of Jesus'
synagogue preaching and healing ministry has now given place (beginning
at Mark 3:7) to a similar ministry, in the open spaces. The increasing
crowds and the opposition which had intensified on the part of the Jewish
religious authorities, mainly brought this about:

• Jesus was accused of blasphemy (Mark 2:7)
• Jesus was accused of being mad (Mark 3:21)
• Jesus was accused of sorcery (Mark 3:22).

It is at this crucial stage in the ministry of Jesus that Mark introduces the
graphic scene where our Lord addresses a huge crowd of people from a
small fishing boat on the Galilean lakeside. It is quite possible that as Jesus
was addressing the crowd a farmer was busy sowing his seed on the
adjacent hillside. Ancient Palestinian agricultural procedure meant that the
farmer would stride out onto his unploughed field, scattering generously
the seed. It would then be ploughed into the ground.

The first-century Palestinian farmer would not consider his sowing a
wasted effort if he had a harvest of between seven and ten per cent yield.
This would be considered a good average yield. Such a poor harvest in the
twenty-first century would be considered catastrophic.

Let us look into the mirror of this parable and learn to apply the lessons
Jesus is seeking to teach us. The real question in regard to this important
parable is: Where is the emphasis of its message? The farmer? The seed
and the harvest? The soil? What kind of soil am I?

It comes as no surprise to find the disciples themselves seeking out Jesus
for an explanation of the parable (v. 10).

Peace

'Peace I leave with you; my peace I give you' (v. 27).

Too often we think of peace in a shallow way, imagining it to be merely the absence or cessation of strife. When a war ends, the newspapers will print headlines about peace breaking out! The same when a trade union strike is over! Peace in this sense may mean no more than an uneasy truce or a stalemate, a stand-off.

This is not what the New Testament means by peace. When Jesus, about to face death, told his disciples, 'Peace I leave with you', was he making them a passive bequest of simply no conflict, no strife? Was he handing on an uneasy spiritual truce? Nothing of the kind! He was granting to them a gift so infinitely precious that no one else in all creation could give it.

It is offered now to you as a fruit of the Holy Spirit. It is the priceless experience of being in a right relationship with God, with yourself, and hence with others. It is a very positive thing. It is harmony. It is God striking the right chords within you so that you feel at ease with yourself – not complacent; just content to be you and glad to be a steadily growing follower of the Lord. Only a person thus at ease can be relaxed and in harmony with others. The Hebrew greeting, *shalom*, comes close to this idea, wishing another the experience of a life in harmony.

'Peace' is also a Christian greeting. It is Christ's resurrection greeting (John 20:19, 21). It is in fact a common New Testament greeting. Check this in the opening verses of, for example, Romans and Galatians. Notice where the peace comes from: 'from God our Father and from the Lord Jesus Christ'. For you it is mediated from the same divine sources through the gentle, courteous ministrations of the Holy Spirit.

You cannot win peace by struggling for it or grasping after it. As with all the fruits of the Spirit, it is given, not seized. It is received, not achieved. And like joy, it can exist and continue in the believer despite trouble. Christ is our peace (Ephesians 2:14). So as you pray to know more of Christ and of his indwelling, your knowledge and experience of his peace will deepen.

Patience

'Love is patient' (1 Corinthians 13:4).

Being patient is probably one of the most elusive of the fruits of the Spirit. Some people are patient by nature. However, the Bible is referring to God, through the Holy Spirit, placing within the believer something of his own divine longsuffering and forbearance.

Putting this in day-to-day practical terms, the fruit of divine patience in you, perhaps only a tiny glimmer at first, will curtail your short-temperedness. It will, through God's grace, keep you steady under provocation. The patient Christian is one who holds back from exasperation or retaliation whereas before he would not. God has been like this with you in waiting patiently to win you to himself. In Romans 2:4, Paul writes of God's 'kindness, tolerance and patience' in leading us to repent.

This aspect of God's character is vividly brought out by Jesus in his story of the lost and wayward son in Luke 15. The real hero of the story is the father, who represents God. He waited patiently for his foolish son to come home (the son represents you and me) and welcomed him lovingly when the time came.

To this divine fruit of patience growing in the personality of a naturally impatient person is a sure indication that the Holy Spirit is at work in that person. So pray (patiently!) for more of this fruit from God. Then you will be 'completely humble and gentle', you will be 'bearing with one another in love' (Ephesians 4:1–2). Notice here the link with love. Again, love is the ground of all the fruit of the Spirit, for 'love is patient'.

Kindness

'Be kind and compassionate to one another' (v. 32).

Not only is love patient, love is also kind according to 1 Corinthians 13:4. Being kind, at the insistence of the Holy Spirit, is therefore not about indulging others or pandering to their wants and wishes. It is rather to discern their needs and to respond in a way best suited to their long-term betterment.

Paul, in Ephesians 4:32, sees a close connection between kindness and being 'compassionate' – that is, sensitive to the needs of others, and even to their weaknesses so that kindness will flow over into forgiveness if necessary. It is worth looking at the broader context of Ephesians 4:32 because it paints a picture of the Christian life, showing what must go out and what should come in when we follow Jesus. The following things have to go:

> Worthless, futile thoughts (v. 17); stubbornness, or hardness of heart (v. 18); vice and all sorts of indecent things (v. 19); the old self (v. 22); deceitful desires (v. 22); telling lies (v. 25); anger that leads into sin (v. 26); giving the devil a foothold (v. 27); theft (v. 28); harmful, unwholesome words (v. 29); offending the Holy Spirit (v. 30); bitterness, rage, anger (v. 31); insults and hateful feelings (malice) (v. 31).

Which of us could manage such a cleansing for ourselves? A spring clean like this is a task for the Holy Spirit, who alone can then add to our lives the following adornments:

> The life that God gives (v. 18); the truth that is in Jesus (v. 21); a new mind (v. 23); the new self (v. 24); God's likeness (v. 24); the true life that is holy and righteous (v. 24); telling the truth (v. 25); working for an honest living (v. 28); helping the poor and needy (v. 28); helpful and encouraging words (v. 29); kindness, tender-heartedness and compassion (v. 32); forgiveness (v. 32).

Goodness

'That by his power he may fulfil every good purpose of yours' (v. 11).

Sometimes we meet a person who is filled with goodness. Catherine Baird was a Salvation Army writer and poet. My wife and I were her neighbours and got to know her well. She would never in a million years have claimed to be good. But she was!

There was something that was godly about her, but it came across in anything but a pious way. She was thoroughly realistic about people and their foibles, yet seemed able to love and accept all types. Everyone felt accepted, even esteemed, by her. This made you want to be a better person – and that is precisely the effect Jesus had on people. So Christ's Spirit was in Catherine Baird, making her good and godly.

She was given also to acts of personal kindness. I think of this when I read the definition of goodness by a former Salvation Army world leader, General Frederick Coutts, who said goodness is 'love with its sleeves rolled up'.

Catherine Baird also laughed a lot. Her eyes laughed, sometimes knowingly, even mischievously, but somehow you knew that from deep within there came welling up a joy and goodness that was of God.

I've offered this brief pen-portrait of a Christian lady because goodness is easier to describe than to define. We know it when we meet it. It flows from the Holy Spirit (Galatians 5:22). He will fulfil, by his power, every desire in us for goodness. This is a crucial promise found in 2 Thessalonians 1:11. Take hold of it as you pray in faith. You belong to Jesus and so you are capable, in a gradually increasing way, of letting your life be 'a rich harvest of every kind of goodness' (Ephesians 5:9, *GNB*). The world needs your life to be like that.

Faithfulness

'The Lord is faithful' (v. 3).

Some translations of the Bible say simply 'faith' or 'fidelity' in Galatians 5:22. The *Jerusalem Bible* has 'trustfulness' and this gets close to the core idea of reliability and trustworthiness that is found in this fruit of the Spirit. Someone said that God does not require brilliance or success, but simply our faithfulness. How reassuring to understand this! This insight helped me a lot in my younger years and still does today.

Like all the fruit we are considering, faithfulness springs from God. 'The Lord is faithful,' declares Paul in 2 Thessalonians 3:3. Specifically, he is faithful 'to strengthen you and keep you safe from the Evil One' (*GNB*). This is underlined in Hebrews 2:17–18 where Jesus is described as faithful and able to help those who are tempted.

So faithfulness in you consists of the Holy Spirit helping to make and keep you consistent in your faith and in your Christian service. No stopping and starting all the time. No letting others down by inconsistency.

Faithfulness, in the sense of loyalty, becomes a key requirement if a position of leadership or responsibility in the congregation is to come your way. 'It is required that those who have been given a trust must prove faithful' (1 Corinthians 4:2). Read Revelation 2:10 and note the prize that is at stake for being faithful to the Lord. My prayer is that one day this prize will be yours.

Meekness

'I am gentle and humble in heart' (v. 29).

Never fall into the trap of mistaking meekness for weakness. The *NIV* says 'gentleness'. In other translations you will find 'humility' used instead of 'meekness', but meekness is exactly the right word. A meek person is not a weak person. Moses was meek, more meek than anyone else alive according to the Bible, yet he was one of the greatest figures in the Old Testament! The *NIV* describes him as 'a very humble man'. Again, we ought not to confuse humility with weakness.

If you pray to be clothed with meekness you are asking God to make you teachable. It has nothing to do with being timid! There are some memorable promises in Scripture for the meek. Psalm 37:11 has them inheriting the earth, and Jesus repeated this (Matthew 5:5) as though to reinforce it. Psalm 149:4 says the Lord will honour (*KJV*: 'beautify') the meek. So it would appear there is some point to this meekness thing after all!

Jesus spoke of his own meekness when he invited men and women to come to him if they were heavily burdened. Out of his meekness he offered, and still offers, rest (Matthew 11:28–29). 'I am gentle and humble [meek] in heart,' he said. In other words, he is not high and mighty in spirit.

I wonder if this would be a good definition of being meek – not being high and mighty in spirit. It may be of use to you to think of it in this way, especially as you pray about this fruit in your own life and attitudes. Your maturing into real meekness will save you from ever thinking you know best all the time or that there is nothing you can be taught. The absence of meekness in a Christian is a very unattractive thing and suggests a measure of spiritual poverty.

One last suggestion about meekness. The Greek word at the root of the concept can mean 'soothing', so think of your meekness being used by the Holy Spirit to affect others like a soothing ointment affects a wound or sting. Perhaps we can say that a meek person is one who can take the heat, or sting, out of a situation. I like this idea and am kneeling with you in prayer for more meekness from God for both of us.

An Abundant Harvest (2):
What Kind of Soil Am I?

'What do you make of this? A farmer planted seed. As he scattered the seed, some of it fell on the road . . . Some fell on good earth' (Mark 4:3, 4, 8, MSG).

As we look into the mirror of this important parable, let us continue to learn to apply its lessons and teaching to our personal lives. We might say, 'If the cap fits wear it.' All listeners need to hear and truthfully examine their own hearts.

The hard soil represents the closed mind, the unteachable spirit – the birds quickly eat up the wasted seed. This is a common occurrence on Australian country roads, especially when trucks freighting grain to storage silos have a spillage on the roadside. A familiar sight is scores of parrots eating the wasted seed.

There is nothing more tragic in life than the person of a closed, unteachable mind and spirit who cannot or will not hear what is being said.

The shallow soil represents the short-lived enthusiasts. *The Message* paraphrases verses 5 and 6: 'They first hear the Word, they respond with great enthusiasm. But there is such shallow soil of character that when the emotions wear off and some difficulty arrives, there is nothing to show for it.'

There is an urgent need for Christians to cultivate the good fertile receptive soil of their hearts and minds:

- By grasping what we believe as Christians
- By the daily discipline of prayer and the study of God's Word
- By growth in Christlikeness
- By sinking deep roots – laying a firm sound foundation for our character. (Echoes here of Jesus' teaching in his parable of the two builders: one built on rock, sinking the foundation deep, and the other built superficially on sand.)

How do we measure up to these requirements?

43

Self-control

'That grace instructs us to . . . live self-controlled, upright, and godly lives'
(Titus 2:12, GNB).

Self-control for a Christian is really God-control, for we are meant to yield every aspect of ourselves and of our lives to him. But the New Testament's choice is to refer to self-control. It means restraining certain natural impulses: temper, a tendency to laziness, bodily appetites for food, sex, etc., overspending on ourselves, or any form of selfishness. It is not hard to think of other examples. Self-control is the opposite of self-indulgence, or unhealthy over-indulgence. Sometimes it is spoken of as temperance or moderation, not being given to silly or extravagant extremes.

Strangely enough, when Paul the apostle appeared before Governor Felix at Caesarea, falsely accused of starting a riot, he chose to debate with Felix, among other things, the merits of self-control (v. 25). His broad theme was faith in Jesus Christ (v. 24) and it is noteworthy that he saw 'goodness' and 'self-control' (v. 25) as being at the heart of the practical results of believing in Jesus. No wonder it was at this point that Felix called the trial proceedings to a halt! Paul's words must have begun to strike home.

Self-control is singled out in the New Testament as especially called for in the following persons (see Titus 1 and 2): church elders (1:8); older Christian men (2:2); younger Christian women (2:5); younger Christian men (2:6); all Christians! (2:12). So, nobody is left out. Self-control is a normative aspect of Christian living.

The self-controlled life is also an 'upright' and 'godly' life (Titus 2:12). Resist the temptation to think self-control in this sense can be self-induced. It can't. Like all the fruits of the Spirit it is from God. How is it received? How are any of the fruits received? On one's knees. Even a small child knows that if they want something they should ask for it. You are God's child. Ask. Ask in faith.

Question Time

This series is collated from chapters in Question Time, *by Major Clifford Kew. The book, published by The Salvation Army's United Kingdom Territory in 1997, looks at Jesus' teaching on citizenship in the kingdom of God as recorded in Matthew's Gospel. The focus is on questions asked by Jesus, by his disciples, and by the Jewish and Roman authorities.*

Introduction

Asking questions (and being asked questions) is one of the most important of educational methods. They are asked in order to establish a starting point; to create atmosphere; to identify problems; to encourage participation and interchange; to stimulate interest and motivation; to collect information; to focus thinking; to develop thought; to direct discovery; to test knowledge and understanding; and to apply truth. We shall find all these principles occurring in our study of the questions asked by and of Jesus.

It is not surprising that particular questions had to be asked, or that so many were so difficult to answer, or that the answers are not always easy to comprehend. The life and teaching of Jesus demanded one of the greatest revolutions of all time in religious thinking, a revolution which reached a breakneck rate of change in the last days of Jesus' ministry.

The crux of all his teaching was the kingdom of heaven, and that is where our emphasis will lie, as the titles of the daily meditations will show. This is the same as the kingdom of God (the term used in other Gospels) and is not to be limited to another life in the future but includes the rule of God in the hearts and minds of believers here and now.

Examining the questions and answers, we may well find – indeed, perhaps we ought to find – that we are far short of allowing the complete operation of the kingdom in our lives.

Greatness in the Kingdom

'At that time the disciples came to Jesus and asked, "Who is the greatest in the kingdom of heaven?"' (v. 1).

It is strange that the subject of 'greatness' came up at all in the company of disciples. Neither their master nor they had much in the way of qualifications for greatness in the usual sense. They were not high-born or wealthy, nor did they come from positions of great influence or power. They were for the most part poor provincials and unlearned. Their work was generally routine. They were not even well-versed in religious theory or practice, certainly no more than the average Jew. And yet they seem to have aspired to greatness.

Perhaps, however, they were not thinking of greatness as a largeness of spiritual experience and influence or as a width or depth of ability, so much as a supremacy of position and authority, and lesser men are not exempt from such desires. They wanted Jesus to establish a pecking order among members of the kingdom and hoped to be near the top of it. They may have been ambitious for power rather than purity and usefulness.

Are we not often concerned with being 'somebody' rather than being 'something', focusing on our status instead of our character? What are we really ambitious for?

The essence of the kingdom is reality, and the more we indulge in pretence, posture, position and pride, the more difficult it will be for us to find any place in it, let alone the highest place. Jesus makes it clear that this involves a deliberate change in adult behaviour: 'Unless *you* change and *become*' (v. 3). But Jesus says the opposite: 'Unless you change and become like little children, you will never enter the kingdom of heaven.'

As disciples, we are all in the infants' class. Yet none of this is to say that we should be childish. We are not to be Peter Pans who never grow up. Paul says: 'When I become a man, I put childish ways behind me' (1 Corinthians 13:11). It is not the immaturity of the child that we seek but its innocence and its integrity.

Mission in the Kingdom

'What do you think? If a man owns a hundred sheep, and one of them wanders away, will he not leave the ninety-nine on the hills and go to look for the one that wandered off?' (v. 12).

Leave all for the sake of one? Surely Jesus is not encouraging us to neglect the flock we already have under our control. He is not saying that shepherds of the Christian flock should neglect those who are already members of the flock and let them wander off also. The shepherd in the parable was pretty sure that the ninety-nine were all right where they were, so that he could give all his attention to the emergency of the lost one, so that it may be brought back to where it belongs.

The point is that the man was not just a farmer, but a shepherd. He was concerned not just about the total or average yield per acre, but also was dealing with individual living animals, whose names he knew, and who knew his voice. They were not just mutton to him, so one of them meant more to him than its weight in dead meat.

The shepherd is not just an administrator but a pastor. He is not dealing in commodities (meat) but in individuals (sheep). The Christian pastor is concerned not just about the totality of his congregation but with people as people. And if one goes off the rails his first priority will be to get him back on track.

Jesus is telling us that there is a need for both ministry and mission in the Church. We must never be content merely with what we have to hand. We must be ready to go out and bring others in, and the emergency situation of those in immediate danger demands that they sometimes have to have priority.

Today, it seems there are more lost than safe in the fold. So the priority for rounding up the lost may be even more urgent. But the joy of redemption is even greater than the joy of keeping in the fellowship those who are there already. This is not a priority of love for the lost, but a priority of necessary action.

Forgiveness in the Kingdom

'Lord, how many times shall I forgive my brother when he sins against me? Up to seven times?' . . . 'Shouldn't you have had mercy on your fellow-servant just as I had on you?' (vv. 21, 33).

Many people, perhaps most people, would find it difficult even to reach Peter's standard of forgiving seven times. If the same person does the same thing to you repeatedly, it takes a good deal of charity to forgive even that often. So by ordinary standards, Peter was far from unforgiving when he 'thought of a number'. But when Jesus says 490 times is nearer the mark, he is not saying that we may keep a tally and stop forgiving when we get to 491. He is using this large number as a symbol of infinity – you should never stop forgiving however much you have forgiven up to now.

As Jesus' love has no limits, so it should be with our forgiving. His mention of seventy-times-seven is to be understood not as setting a more generous limit, but in a symbolic way (seven being a symbolic number in the thinking of the day), meaning, 'There is no limit. The sky's the limit!'

Of course, in another sense, you never even get to forgiving seven times, because if you truly forgive you wipe the slate clean. The placing of any limit is a misunderstanding of the nature of forgiveness. This clean slate is of the very nature of forgiving. If we truly are forgiving, we will not add up the slights and hurts and deeper wounds that occur in every life, and each time an offence occurs, the slate is always wiped clean.

The parable (vv. 23–34) reminds us that it is easier to be forgiven than to forgive, but if we do not forgive, we cannot expect to be forgiven. And this applies not only to our dealings with other people but also to our relationship with God.

The second question highlighted in today's reading (v. 33) gives us one of the most straightforward reasons for forgiveness and for persistence in forgiveness. Our forgiveness ought to reflect the pattern of God's forgiveness of us. And it is not only in the *number* of pardons that we must be like God, but in the *nature* of that mercy – unrecorded, unconditional and unlimited.

The Law in the Kingdom (1)

'Some Pharisees came to him to test him. They asked, "Is it lawful for a man to divorce his wife for any and every reason?" "Haven't you read . . . ?" he replied' (vv. 3–4).

The original question asked of Jesus is not whether divorce is ever legitimate, but whether divorce *for any* and *every reason* is allowable (the *Good News Bible* says 'for whatever reason he wishes'). Not even modern Western society allows divorce on those grounds.

Several points should be noticed to aid correct interpretation here. First, the Pharisees were hostile listeners (v. 3). They were again trying to trap Jesus, and so he may have had to give a more guarded answer than he might have given in other circumstances. Second, he turned the question back on them for they knew the law (v. 4). And the law of Moses did allow divorce. The Pharisees were quite right in saying that (Deuteronomy 24: 1–4; Matthew 5: 31–32), and Jesus did not countermand it, only enlarged on the nature of true Christian marriage.

But the Pharisees were experts in splitting hairs and had made divorce so easy that the rabbi Hillel cites a case of divorce on the grounds that the wife put too much salt in the soup. They were concerned to establish a *minimum* standard for marriage. Likewise, some people today seek to define how little goodness they can get away with.

What Jesus was always interested in was a spiritual understanding of what true marriage is all about (vv. 4–6). He is not interested in minimum standards in marriage – as perverted by those who want only to lower standards – but in model marriage as intended by God. True Christians are always concerned 'to be the best that I can be' (*SASB* 860, v. 3) rather than to be only as good as will ensure (they think) their own salvation.

49

The Law in the Kingdom (2)

' "Why then," they asked, "did Moses command that a man give his wife a certificate of divorce and send her away?" ' (v. 7).

What Jesus says when pressed is that the law does allow divorce, because men's hearts are so sinful, but that there is one allowable ground for divorce and that is marital unfaithfulness. Here (v. 9) and in Matthew 5:31–32 he says divorce *on other grounds* means that remarriage should be seen as adultery in the case of all parties.

Even so, we should beware of going further than Jesus, even in his condemnation of adultery and divorce. When he met a woman who had had five husbands (presumably not all dead) and was even then 'living in sin', Jesus not only met her spiritual need but also allowed her to be the means of evangelising her whole village (John 4: 17–18, 25, 28–30). And when he came across a crowd carrying out the strict letter of the law on adultery, by stoning to death an adulterous woman, he delivered her from the crowd and his judgment on her was simply, 'Go now and leave your life of sin' (John 8:3–11).

Neither adultery nor divorce is the unforgivable sin and we, like Jesus, must be willing to allow people to benefit from the gospel of the second chance. He disapproved but did not excommunicate. On the basis of Scripture, then, the *most* we can insist on is no divorce without adultery; not, no divorce.

But Matthew 19:5–6 surely allows the possibility that when a married couple are no longer, or may even never have been, 'one flesh' as God intended, we may have to allow divorce, even for other reasons, when the God-intended 'blessed estate of matrimony' is not being realised. We do not have to conclude that the compassionate Jesus would deny for ever to those who make a tragic mistake in first marriage any hope of a second marriage conceived by the principles of verses 4–6.

What Jesus is really condemning is not so much divorce whatever the circumstance, but a casual attitude to marriage and remarriage, which involves just as serious issues as adultery within marriage. Such 'easy come, easy go' attitudes are a contravention of the spirit of true marriage, and perhaps just as bad as adultery.

An Abundant Harvest (3):

The Crowded Soil

*'The desires for other things come in and choke the word,
making it unfruitful' (v. 19).*

This soil represents those who are torn by distracting and competing interests. 'These are the people who hear the message, but the worries of this world and the false glamour of riches . . . creep in and choke the life out of what they have heard' (vv. 18–19, *JBP*).

The snare of worldliness and materialism is poignantly demonstrated in the life of Demas. Paul mentions Demas several times as an enthusiastic Christian worker. Sadly, we learn from the apostle that his fellow-worker Demas has been caught in the snare of worldliness: 'Demas, because he loved this world, has deserted me' (2 Timothy 4:10).

From this fellow-worker with the great apostle Paul we learn a timely lesson and warning. Am I becoming too caught up in my lifestyle to have time to worship God and serve him?

The Good Soil

*'The seed in good soil represents those who bring a good and honest
heart to the hearing of the word, hold it fast, and by their
perseverance yield a harvest' (Luke 8:15, NEB).*

Here we find the grain is buried and germinates in the good soil. This represents the open and receptive mind and heart. The key is the Greek word *hupomone*. It means a person maintains their faith with steadfastness; in contrast to the closed-mind hearer; the rootless superficial hearer; the choked mind and distracted hearer.

On the other hand, the righteous in the teaching of Jesus are characterised by the steadfastness and persistence with which they cling to their faith and service in spite of opposition and severe temptation.

Jesus is teaching in his parable that in spite of all the hazards and failures, God's reign advances as the harvest exceeds all expectations.

Goodness in the Kingdom

'"Teacher, what good thing must I do to get eternal life?" "Why do you ask me about what is good?" Jesus replied. "... If you want to enter life, obey the commandments"' (vv. 16–18).

The rich young man's original question may betray a wrong attitude. Maybe he looks at goodness in ledger terms. How many good deeds can he enter on the credit side to balance out any debits? He can do good turns from the loftiness of his self-esteem and the security of his wealth, without it really costing him too much. He concentrates on 'doing' to build up recognition for himself and a credit rating in heaven.

But will it change him as a person? Will it really make him good in his inmost being? There can be a difference between making a good impression and acting in love. There is a world of difference between a religion of law and a religion of grace.

When Jesus speaks of keeping the commandments, the young man wants specifics: 'Which ones?' (v. 18). Is there a choice? Can we make our own selection and make ourselves good just by keeping to that restricted morality? The young man wants a definition of *minimum* standards. He wants eternal life, and feels he has paid enough for it by his moral life, but he wants to be certain. Verse 16 seems to sum up his basic attitude: 'What ... must I do to get?' He looks on eternal life as just one more acquisition. Even eternal life can be the object of selfish desire.

In fact, Jesus cites only five of the ten commandments (vv. 18–19), and sums them up in the words, 'Love your neighbour as yourself.' Is this significant or does he just take these as samples of all the commandments? It is of interest that all five are in the second half of the commandments – those that refer to relationships between man and man, rather than between man and God. The young man had kept all these. Was the thing that he lacked to be found, then, in the area of his relationship to God? Was it that he had made wealth his god, and so was in breach of the first commandment: 'You shall have no other gods before me' (Exodus 20:3)?

It may not be wealth that is the obstacle in our case, but whatever is dear to us must be secondary to Christ in our affections.

Rewards in the Kingdom

'When the disciples heard this, they were greatly astonished and asked,
"Who then can be saved?" . . . Peter answered him, ". . . What then
will there be for us?"' (vv. 25, 27).

After the departure of the rich young ruler, Jesus warned the disciples that 'it is hard' for a rich man to enter the kingdom of God. Hard but not impossible! The word picture Jesus used to illustrate this difficulty may suggest that it's impossible. A camel through the eye of a needle? Never! But there was sometimes in the walls of ancient cities a little gate beside the main gate. When the main gate was closed at night, the only way in was by the pedestrian gate at the side – sometimes called the Needle's Eye. A man could get through there at night but not his camel and baggage as well. He would have to leave his possessions behind.

So though it is hard for a rich man to enter the kingdom, perhaps the suggestion is that it's not impossible if he is willing to shed the encumbrances of his possessions, to give away the burden of his wealth. So what seems impossible from a human point of view is possible if God is put in his proper place (v. 26). Salvation is based on a loving relationship, not a commercial bargain.

The disciples' question, 'Who then can be saved?' shows that they too were still preoccupied with wealth and position. If a rich ruler couldn't be saved, who could be? Jesus' teaching was a charter for the common man. The criteria for acceptance in the world are not the same as those for acceptance in the kingdom of God. Sadly, we allow ourselves to be brainwashed into thinking that status, security and selfishness are preferable to salvation and sanctification.

In the second question (v. 27), however, Peter sees himself and the other disciples as being in the opposite situation. They have given up everything to follow Jesus, but is there not a smidgen of the same self-centred spirit as that of the rich man when Peter asks, 'What is there in it for us?' Peter thought self-sacrifice would guarantee returns. Was he thinking of possessions or position? What we need most is soul satisfaction and spiritual status as a child of God – the spiritual security of his love.

Equality in the Kingdom

'He asked them, "Why have you been standing here all day long doing nothing?" . . . "Didn't you agree to work for a denarius?"' (vv. 6, 13).

This parable sets out to illustrate the last statement of the previous chapter, 'Many who are first will be last, and many that are last will be first', a principle that is repeated in verse 16. But really it teaches that all will be treated equally. Whatever the contribution to the kingdom, the rewards will be the same.

The landowner asks the men who were hired last, 'Why have you been standing here all day long doing nothing?' Silly question! They probably *have* been doing something essential all day – looking for work, waiting in the marketplace, the job centre, to be hired, without which they would have no income.

It may well have been that those who appeared in the marketplace late in the day had been trudging all day from one village to another seeking work. They were certainly persistent and thought that an hour's work was better than nothing. (Others might have given up and gone home.) It is worth noting, however, that there is work for all in the kingdom of God. 'The field is the world' (Matthew 13:38) and opportunities for serving God are limitless.

The second question in the story is asked when it comes to the pay-out and it is asked of the men hired *first* (v. 14). Isn't it natural for men who have worked all day to expect more in their wage packet than those who have worked for an hour? Natural, yes, but there is at least *justice* on the landowner's side. They got what they had been promised. God cannot give us *more* than eternal life, whatever we do to 'earn' it.

The first-comers got what they *needed*. The late-comers' needs were just as great, so they all got the same reward. To repeat, God treats us according to need not deserts. Of course, we must not have the attitude of doing as little as possible to warrant our inclusion in the kingdom, but these men had not done as little as possible but as much as they could.

Position in the Kingdom

'Can you drink the cup I am going to drink?' (v. 22).

Today's reading begins with the third statement by Jesus concerning his passion – how it would all end. He could not have been more explicit, but the only response of the disciples was to squabble over jobs for the boys. They weren't thinking along the right lines at all. Their minds were filled with their own concerns, their own ambitions.

Jesus asks James and John, 'Can you drink the cup I am going to drink?' and they glibly respond, 'We can.' They were over-confident. Spiritual maturity may make us *less* confident of our own ability at the same time as making us *more* committed to God's will. Their willingness to commit themselves, without understanding or thought, to sharing the lot of Christ showed that they had still much to learn, in spite of repeated warnings.

Jesus tells them that they will get their second wish if not their first. They will have to 'drink from my cup', to undergo struggle, suffering and sacrifice for the kingdom (without being assured of position or prestige in the kingdom thereafter).

The disciples were playing the wrong game, so taken up by their own little concerns that they did not bother to take note of Jesus' great concerns. They were thinking in terms of worldly ambition, not just in the work of discipleship but also in terms of Jesus' coming kingdom. At a time when Jesus' mind was full of the cup of suffering, their minds were full of the crowns they wanted to wear – personal prominence, personal reward, personal distinction, personal success – rather than the cup of personal sacrifice they might have to sip.

How often is it true of us that we are playing our own game which does not fit in with the serious business that Jesus is about? When he takes a different direction, we try to persuade him that our way is best – and failing, as fail we must, we wander off on our own.

Jesus calls us mostly to ordinary service, not to outstanding position and spectacular achievement.

Compassion in the Kingdom

' "*What do you want me to do for you?*" *he asked*' (v. 32).

It is significant that the question Jesus asked the two blind men in Jericho was very similar to the one asked of the mother of James and John (see yesterday's reading – 20:21). But there is at least an implied difference. 'What is it you want?' is a general question which the disciples interpreted in terms of favour. Here, Jesus asks, 'What do you want me to do for you?' – a more restricted and particular question.

It was because the men realised their real need and pitched their prayer at the point of real need that Jesus had compassion, touched their eyes and restored their sight. Their plea was for basic equipment for life, not for the trimmings of personal aggrandisement.

Another difference is in the approach of the blind men. Here the blind men come asking not for justice or reward but for mercy, and they address Jesus as Lord and Messiah (v. 30). Our prayers are more likely to be answered if we come reverently and worshipfully, and ask for gifts of grace, not reward.

It is no part of Christian compassion to give people always what they want. This may be the way to foster arrogance (as it would have been with James and John), or to foster sloth and unnecessary dependence (perhaps in the case of those who could support themselves if they tried). However, it is very easy to be hard-headed about the needs of others – to say that the state should not allow it, or that society should prevent it, or that the individual should do more for himself. But for the Christian such thinking must be balanced with compassion for the individual sufferer.

Real compassion is driven not by a policy but by a purpose, and the purpose must always be the *ultimate* good of those who utter the cry of need, according to the present circumstance.

Jesus' *first* purpose was ministering to the souls of men. He had constantly to struggle to keep that purpose uppermost, but when confronted by a genuine cry of need, which could be met in no other way, his compassion compels him to respond – as with these two blind beggars on the road to Jericho.

Resources in the Kingdom

' "If anyone asks you, 'Why are you doing this?' tell him, 'The Lord needs it' " . . . some people standing there asked, "What are you doing, untying that colt?" ' (Mark 11:3, 5).

We switch from Matthew's Gospel to Mark's account here as these verses are couched more directly in question form in the latter, though the truths which emerge are the same.

The question, first, is why the disciples are commandeering someone else's property; by what authority are they doing this? In view of the 'password' given by Jesus to the disciples (Mark 11:3), it may well be that there was a measure of prearrangement in this, or that the owner was known to Jesus as a devoted follower. But there is a sense in which Jesus is the Lord of all creation and, though he chose to exercise his ministry almost totally without material resources, he has the *right* to commandeer the resources of all those who accept his Lordship.

Jesus had no donkey but the one a follower was willing to lend him. We must make our resources available to him, for he can work through us. We need just to provide the means by which our Master can come to people in the way he deems best, not in the way we would think right.

The wider question, however, is why Jesus was telling them to do this. Why the strange instructions to commandeer a donkey? The donkey was a symbol of peace – a horse for war, a donkey for peace. So this probably prearranged show of authority was a graphic illustration of Jesus' importance, but at the same time it revealed him as a gentle, peaceful king rather than a warrior 'Son of David'.

It is not surprising that the disciples thought their only hope was in a military deliverer. It is perhaps more surprising that they cottoned on, as quickly and as much as they did, to the meaning of the man on a donkey (see Zechariah 9:9).

If we are among the crowd of disciples and pilgrims, we must be aware of the danger of expecting the Lord to come with the kind of earthly power that will put earth's wrongs right in the short term.

An Abundant Harvest (4):

The Farmer, the Seed, the Harvest

*'Stand firm! Let nothing move you as you busy yourselves in the
Lord's work. Be sure that nothing you do for him is ever lost or wasted'
(1 Corinthians 15:58, JBP).*

Jesus teaches this parable in a time of increasing uncertainty, disappointment and difficulty in his mission and ministry. Yet Jesus in this
parable teaches that in spite of much loss, waste, despair, disappointment
and toil, there will be a harvest – an abundant harvest! The farmer did not
stop sowing the seed; in fact he seemed to be extravagantly sowing the
seed, because of the rocky outcrops, the hard-beaten paths, or for that
matter the existence of the weeds and thorns.

It would be true to say that the Christian, the Salvationist, the minister
of the gospel may well see the experience in a lifelong ministry – hard toil,
disappointment, rejection, loss, heartache, disillusionment – and reflect on
why God has permitted such seeming waste of labour and toil in the cause
of Christ and the gospel.

Yet our Lord clearly teaches in this parable that no matter how much
seed may appear to be wasted, there will be a glorious harvest. Matthew's
Gospel brings out this truth most emphatically: 'Other seed fell on good
soil, where it produced a crop – a hundred, sixty or thirty times what was
sown' (13:8).

That represents truly an abundant harvest, keeping in mind that a result
of seven to ten per cent yield would have been considered in those days a
most satisfactory result. The major emphasis and focal point of the parable
proper is to be found in the very large harvest.

Here, then, from the lips of Jesus himself is a ringing call for faith in
God's power to bring his sovereign purposes to their triumphant fulfilment. So often during the course of his earthly ministry, especially when
addressing his disciples, Jesus would exclaim: 'Take heart – be of good
cheer.'

How appropriate and relevant for us today are the apostle Paul's words
in our key text, addressed to the Christians in Corinth. Yes, in the end there
will be a very large harvest.

The Lord in the Kingdom

*'When Jesus entered Jerusalem, the whole city was stirred and asked,
"Who is this?" The crowds answered, "This is Jesus, the prophet
from Nazareth in Galilee" ' (vv. 10–11).*

It must have been difficult for the disciples to stop thinking in terms of a kingdom in which they would have power, and think in terms of one in which they would have only opportunities of service. Christ's power is not the power of an authoritarian dictator or a bully. His power is not a power that treads on the lowliest in order to reach the highest. This is a power that, when it is let loose in the world, will triumph through truth and love.

There is clearly a differentiation in verses 10 and 11 between 'the whole city' and 'the crowds'. 'The whole city' would refer to the permanent residents of Jerusalem, and possibly other people who had arrived for the festival. So it is the people who are already in the city who ask the 'pilgrims' who are escorting Jesus, 'Who is this?' As followers of Jesus, we have a duty to stimulate those who do not know him into asking questions about him. When questions are asked about Jesus' identity, we must be ready with a plain unvarnished answer.

It's interesting to note that the pilgrims did not at first share with the Jerusalemites their instinctive reaction that Jesus was 'the Son of David', the expected conquering hero, or 'the Messiah', someone even greater – the terms they had used on the march. They began with the plain fact: 'Jesus from Nazareth'; but they do add a 'prophet' – and there had been no prophet, apart from John the Baptist, for a couple of hundred years or more, so even that was saying something significant.

The pilgrims somewhat watered down the answer as to who Jesus was. The critical question with regard to Jesus is: 'Who is he?' It's not enough to say 'a prophet', nor even to give him his human identity, 'Jesus of Nazareth in Galilee'. It is only when we complete his identification as Son of David, Messiah – indeed, Son of God – that we have posed the final challenge to the world.

Children in the Kingdom

*' "Do you hear what these children are saying?" they asked him.
"Yes," replied Jesus, "have you never read, 'From the lips of children
and infants you have ordained praise'?" ' (v. 16).*

When Jesus had cleared the traders out of the temple, healed the blind
and the lame, and the children were 'having a ball' with him,
acclaiming him as 'Son of David', the stern and irate chief priests and
teachers of the law asked him, 'Do you hear what these children are
saying? How can you let them utter such blasphemous nonsense?'

In return, Jesus asked them the simplest of questions, based on their
own prized Scriptures: 'Have you never read, "From the lips of children
and infants you have ordained praise"?' Children may not always be
aware of, or restrained by, what adults deem to be appropriate; they may
not understand the ramifications of theology or religious etiquette; but
they know when there is cause to celebrate, to express joy, to utter the
basic wisdom of pure hearts.

But we need to be able to understand the situation from the other side
too. The Sadducees were the guardians of the religious rites of the temple
and also the political leaders of the nation. They did not want anybody to
rock the boat in either area. The scribes were the religious intelligentsia.

We ourselves must beware of being stern spoilsports simply in order to
maintain our own conveniences or prejudices. We should be on the side of
the children, however difficult we may find that temperamentally. We need
to share the spontaneity, joy, worship and wisdom of all that is best in
children. Instead of indoctrinating children with adult fears, adult greed,
adult hatreds, we would do well to listen to their views about war, the
environment, the poor and so on.

Radio and television shows featuring children's views often surprise us
with their freshness and perspicacity. When eleven-year-old cancer victim
Jamie Bowen (whose father insisted on treatment even after the local health
authority refused to fund it as likely to be ineffective) was questioned by
the experienced interviewer Robert Kilroy-Silk, he was prompted to ask,
'Where did you get such wisdom?'

In this sense, to be like a child is not to be gullible or unreasoning but to
be simple. It is not a retrogressive step out of adulthood, but a forward step
into wisdom.

Judgment in the Kingdom

' "How did the fig-tree wither so quickly?" they asked' (v. 20).

Jesus was walking from his base in the village of Bethany towards the Jerusalem city centre, when he stopped beside a fig-tree. Actually it seems that Jesus was looking for figs when there couldn't be any (edible ones at least). It was too early in the year (April). So Jesus appears to curse the tree for not doing what was impossible anyway, and to do so for his own ends too – because he was hungry.

It may be that Jesus had discerned that there was something wrong with the tree, and so he said, 'It will never bear fruit.' To a discerning countryman's eye it would be clear that the tree was doomed. This may have been another pictorial way of Jesus saying that Judaism might look sound, but its true present state foretold disaster. The tree had leaves and looked healthy, but it would produce no fruit. There was a good profession but no fruition. Perhaps Jesus was using the fig-tree (as it often had been used in the Old Testament) as a symbol of the Jewish nation, and saying that it would wither because of its lack of fruitfulness.

We will have difficulty with this story if we regard it as a 'nature miracle'. It will then seem a rather bad-tempered and destructive act on the part of Jesus, especially viewing it from these days of environmental concern. It seems out of character for Jesus to put a blight on nature. Perhaps, then, like the triumphal entry to Jerusalem, it is more of a dramatically illustrated parable, this time about judgment in the kingdom of God.

According to John's Gospel, Jesus said (at about the same point in his ministry – in Holy Week): 'Neither can you bear fruit unless you remain in me . . . If anyone does not remain in me, he is like a branch that is thrown away and withers; such branches are picked up, thrown into the fire and burned' (John 15:4, 6). So this action of cursing the fig-tree means that judgment is inescapable. Discipleship means fruitfulness, and lack of fruit presages disaster.

We should realise that the curse Jesus appears to have put on the tree is to be understood as an example neither of how we should pray nor of an act of faith. It was just a demonstration of truth. But in these verses Jesus tells the disciples that, in contrast to the fruitlessness of the fig-tree, faith is the secret of fruitfulness.

Authority in the Kingdom

' "*By what authority are you doing these things?" they asked. "And who gave you this authority?" Jesus replied, "I will also ask you one question . . . John's baptism – where did it come from? Was it from heaven, or from men?"* ' (vv. 23–25).

There were eleven chief priests in addition to the high priest, and they were the ruling nucleus of the Sanhedrin (a council of seventy members). They were members of prominent priestly families who regarded themselves as the supreme authority in Judaism (under the Roman conquerors), and were the guardians of the temple, controlling the direction of the daily services and the administration of its massive finances. They regarded all religious activity as their province. They had not given Jesus licence to preach and perform miracles, so under what authority did he act?

Jesus' return question about John the Baptist and his authority is not a diversion or an excuse to evade their questions. He is finding out whether they have a basic comprehension of what spiritual authority means, so he asks for their reaction to the other great spiritual figure of the time – John the Baptist. He had not received authority or approval from them. Yet he was a popular figure, almost universally acknowledged as a prophet.

This put the religious leaders on the horns of a dilemma. If they admitted the authority of John, they had to admit the authority of Jesus, to whom John had pointed as 'the Lamb of God'. So they hummed and hawed, and in the end gave a non-committal answer.

It was obvious, therefore, that they could not or would not see that spiritual authority comes not from earthly institutions or establishment figures, but from God. And if they didn't understand that, there was no prospect of them understanding or accepting that Jesus was not even a prophet, but Messiah, Son of God. They were not prepared to allow for the possibility of any greater authority than their own, so that when a figure of greater innate spiritual authority did appear, they could only set themselves up in opposition to him.

The danger that they may come to obstruct the workings of God himself is always present in religious structures, organisations and authorities. But these established institutions must be avenues for the moving of the Holy Spirit, not restrictions upon his work.

Obedience in the Kingdom

'Which of the two did what his father wanted?' (v. 31)

Neither of these boys was an ideal son. The ideal son would have immediately agreed to go and work in the vineyard and would have done so. So neither was entirely satisfactory. But, Jesus says, if it comes to a choice between politeness on the one hand and obedience on the other, give me obedience every time. As Matthew 7:21–23 quotes Jesus:

> Not everyone who says to me, 'Lord, Lord,' will enter the kingdom of heaven, but only he who does the will of my Father who is in heaven. Many will say to me on that day, 'Lord, Lord, did we not prophesy in your name, and in your name drive out demons and perform many miracles?' Then I will tell them plainly, 'I never knew you. Away from me, you evildoers!'

Even religious activities which are not the result of obedience are vain.

The second son may perhaps be taken to represent those who for one reason or another are unwilling to make an open and immediate religious commitment, but nevertheless live according to God's standards. We are not, of course, to assume from this that the ideal disciple is one who first rejects Christ's call but then changes his mind, or one who, like Nicodemus, is a secret disciple and does not confess him openly. It is simply that grudging obedience is better than polite disobedience.

Matthew 23:3 says that the teachers of the law and the Pharisees 'do not practise what they preach'. They say one thing and do another. Both the sons did this, but the ultimately preferred son realised his error and put it right by doing what the father wanted. He responded to the promptings of conscience, however belatedly.

On the other hand, tax collectors and publicans, who previously made no pretence at being godly people, were now responding to the gospel of righteousness which John the Baptist had proclaimed to them. So, in spite of their bad start, they will get into the kingdom, while the religious leaders won't because they never met the condition of obedience.

Perhaps we should assume a third son who both says and does the right thing. We should try to be like that third son.

Punishment in the Kingdom

*'When the owner of the vineyard comes, what will he
do to those tenants?' (v. 40)*

Parables usually have one main point to be grasped, but it seems in this tale of murder among the vines that many of the details have a precise meaning. In this parable the owner is God; the tenants are the Jewish religious leaders; the messengers are the prophets; the son is Jesus. In a sense, the story is autobiographical (v. 39).

Absentee landlords were part of the country scene and sometimes represented injustice, but here the tenants are highlighted and in this case were ruthlessly dishonest. They were prepared to do anything rather than meet their obligations, just as today it seems to be an increasing feature of business life that there are many con men.

We should notice, however, that this owner is patient. He has done everything possible to make the vineyard prosperous – wall, winepress, watchtower and all (v. 33). Similarly, God had created the world and all that is in it for man's benefit; he had given Israel, as his chosen people, every blessing he could.

Even now, the owner does not come down on the tenants like a ton of bricks at their first refusal, but he gives them one chance after another. It is when they finally reject and kill even his own son that action is taken. Mark 12:6 says, 'He had one left to send, a son, whom he loved.' God had given the Jews every chance to respond to his just demands but they had rejected all of them.

No matter how long justice may be delayed by God, it appears that there must come a time when, if righteousness is to have any meaning at all, God must draw the line and deal with those who have persistently refused his overtures to them. We should perhaps note that the particular context of this story is not so much on membership of the kingdom as on leadership in the kingdom. The greater our position in it, the greater our responsibility. The vineyard is God's; he has appointed tenants (leaders) to work it, but if they consistently refuse to give him his due, he must take action for the good of the kingdom.

Excuses! Excuses! (1):

The Great Feast

'Blessed is the man who will eat at the feast in the kingdom of God' (v. 15).

It is to be noted that our Lord's practice of eating in company was a regular and important feature of his earthly ministry. Jesus accepted many invitations to dine with diverse groups as well as individuals – the Pharisees, tax collectors, sinners, and his close disciples and women such as Mary and Martha.

The opening incident, of what was to be a highly charged evening, was Jesus healing, in the presence of a number of scribes (experts in the Torah law – the theologians) and Pharisees, a man suffering with dropsy (vv. 2–6). Following the healing, Jesus observed an embarrassing manoeuvring of a number of the invited guests, rudely positioning themselves in order to secure the most prominent seats at the table. Jesus courageously challenged this inappropriate behaviour by giving a word of advice about attending a banquet (vv. 7–11), concluding with the statement: 'For everyone who exalts himself will be humbled, and he who humbles himself will be exalted' (v. 11).

Jesus then turned his attention to the host of the feast, the local leading Pharisee, giving him advice in regard to the choice of guests to a feast. As a response to this advice given by Jesus, one of the invited guests in a pious outburst said: 'How fortunate the one who gets to eat dinner in God's kingdom!' (v. 15, *MSG*). Such a comment could only have come from a person confident of his own invitation to the great Messianic feast. The comment is a clear reference to a long and passionately held belief and hope within Judaism – the great Messianic feast as prophesied in Isaiah 25:6–8.

Following the pious outburst, Jesus told the gathered guests a parable which would have shaken host and guests to the very foundation of their lives, challenging their pious self-righteousness, complacency and arrogance.

Understanding in the Kingdom

'Jesus said to them, "Have you never read in the Scriptures?"' *(v. 42).*

All three Synoptic Gospels attach this passage to the parable of the tenants in the vineyard, but Matthew's question may suggest a slightly different line of thought to Luke's. 'Have you never read in the Scriptures?' seems to suggest an ignorance of Scripture, which was an oblique insult to the priests and Pharisees, who again 'knew he was talking about them' (v. 45), but who reckoned themselves to be the experts in the knowledge of Scripture. Of course they had read the Scriptures, this very Scripture, but they had not put two and two together and understood that it had any significance as far as Jesus was concerned.

However, Luke's question, 'What, then, does this scripture mean?' (20:17, *GNB*) shows that he is asking them about the particular Scripture which is quoted in Matthew 21:42. It is from Psalm 118:22, where it referred to Israel's key position in the world. It includes the word 'capstone' (*NIV*), the stone that is 'the most important of all' (*GNB*). Israel has failed to fulfil its role, so a new capstone, a new cornerstone, is needed.

So Jesus tells the Jewish religious leaders that they will lose the kingdom because they have not finished erecting the 'royal palace'. There is an eminently suitable stone lying by their feet – Jesus himself, who alone can complete the kingdom. Jesus is the culmination of their faith, but they have rejected him. In our membership of, and especially in our leadership within the kingdom, we need to ensure that Christ is pre-eminent, or we too shall have to be dislodged.

Verse 44 tacks onto this application of the parable (by word association) two other loose stones – the stone of stumbling and the crushing stone – both of which concepts come from Isaiah 8:14–15. So the two disconnected Old Testament passages drawn together by the common word 'stone' teach us that the only way to complete and meaningful faith is when Jesus is crowned as Lord of our lives; but the complementary truth is that we neglect him at our own peril.

Purity in the Kingdom

*'The king . . . noticed a man there who was not wearing wedding clothes.
"Friend," he asked, "how did you get in here without wedding clothes?"
The man was speechless' (vv. 11–12).*

This parable refers to a king in his kingdom preparing a wedding banquet. There is little mention of the wedding itself or the happy couple. It is the guests who are at the centre of the parable – guests of three kinds:

- *The invited guests* – who failed to show up.
- *The replacement guests*. All that was required was willingness, an appetite to receive.
- *The guest without wedding clothes*.

None of these new guests was invited and none had had the chance to dress for the occasion. They had come as they were with no special preparation. It is suggested by some commentators that it often happened in the East that a noble or kingly host provided wedding clothes for the guests to don at the door, and this may be what is in mind here.

If all the other pressed men were in wedding garments they must have been given them as they arrived – which suggests that the improperly dressed guest (v. 11) was in that condition because he simply couldn't be bothered to change, to put on the overgarment. It seems he was only there for the party. He represents those who want to be in the kingdom for the sake of its benefits, but are unwilling to take on the nature of those who inhabit the kingdom.

It would therefore seem that this wedding overgarment represents the garment of holiness, the trademark of which is love. We need to put it on (as Paul suggests in Ephesians 4:22–24 and Colossians 3:9–10) if we are to enter the kingdom. Matthew 22:1–14 states clearly the 'gospel of the open door' – all may enter the kingdom – but that must be balanced by a requirement to have 'a change of clothes' to make us fit to be at the banquet.

There is no good reason for not wearing the wedding garment of purity in the kingdom. It is provided by the grace of God and at the cost of the crucified Son, and it is required by the nature of the fellowship within. We cannot gatecrash the feast, partaking of its benefits without accepting its conditions.

Loyalties in the Kingdom

' "Teacher," they said . . . "What is your opinion? Is it right to pay taxes to Caesar or not?" . . . He asked them, "Whose portrait is this? And whose inscription?" ' (vv. 16–17, 20).

The ideas of the Pharisees and Sadducees were too earthbound; they were more concerned with scoring a point than discovering the truth. And as the crunch point of Jesus' ministry drew near, he had to try to shake his hearers out of this attitude. Their question is a trick but he gives them a serious answer.

The poll tax of a silver piece had been levied by the Romans since AD 6 and was universally detested. The people would have liked Jesus to say, 'Don't pay up', while the Jewish leaders would have been equally pleased because they could then have denounced him to the Romans.

He was between the devil and the deep blue sea. One way he would lose the sympathy of the crowd; the other way he could be charged with sedition. But in his wisdom he found an answer, a clever trap, a reply to which they could not take exception. He dismisses this question on tax liability astutely but firmly, but at the same time points out that obligations towards God must be balanced with obligations towards society. We share the benefits of community life, so we must share the costs.

Politics and religion should not be divorced, but where there is an inescapable conflict, our supreme loyalty must surely be to God. There are occasions when the Church must oppose the state. We are citizens with dual nationality; we owe allegiance both to the world and to the kingdom of heaven. But the final loyalty must lie in the latter.

There are some situations where we will have to agonise over our response to conflicting demands, and finally make a choice on the basis of our very best and clearest motives as guided by the Holy Spirit. This will demand courage as well as wisdom.

Relationships in the Kingdom

' "At the resurrection, whose wife will she be of the seven, since all of them were married to her?" Jesus replied . . . "Have you not read what God said to you?" ' (vv. 28–29, 31).

This is another trick question to which Jesus gives another serious answer. The Sadducees did not believe in resurrection, so they were tongue-in-cheek when they asked it. Their purpose was to ask an unanswerable question and so prove their point.

The question derived from a Deuteronomic custom called Levirate marriage (which seems to have been rarely applied, especially in the time of Jesus) which said that a widow should be taken in marriage by her husband's brother. The Sadducees were posing the even more unlikely hypothesis of it happening over and over again in the same family. If so, whose wife would she be after the resurrection?

Jesus told them that they couldn't distinguish the passing from the permanent. The ideas of the Sadducees were too earthbound, conceived and expressed in terms of time and space. They were thinking of heaven as just a continuation of earthly life, so they ridiculed the eternal reality by caricaturing it. That, however, does not mean that the reality does not exist.

This still leaves us with lots of questions about heaven. Will we know our loved ones? Will we have any special relationship? Jesus does not answer in detail but gives us a general principle and a particular example. The principle is that heaven is a spiritual state, and physical details have no relevance – or only minor relevance – in it. The example is marriage, which will no longer be relevant, at least in its present form. With that we will have to be content, with the assurance that heaven must be about loving relationships, however wide those relationships and however they are expressed.

It is perhaps natural for our restricted human thinking to conceive of heaven in physical terms. The cowboy may think in terms of 'the big ranch in the sky' or the footballer of 'the big stadium in the sky', but we should recognise that this is an indication of our finite minds rather than the infinite spiritual reality of God's provision for us in eternity.

Priorities in the Kingdom

'Teacher, which is the greatest commandment in the Law?' (vv. 35–36).

There is a danger, which we sometimes fall into, that we want to be selective about God's will, to obey him in some things and be self-determining in others. So Jesus would have been on dangerous ground if he had said, for instance, that 'You shall not commit adultery' is more important than 'You shall not steal' (Exodus 20:14–15). You can't pick and choose like that.

Again the long-prepared wisdom of Jesus is seen, in that he did not rise to this bait of discriminating between one specific commandment and another. He selects a verse that is the summing-up of all other commandments (Deuteronomy 6:5). And yet, when Jesus has selected that verse, he is still not quite satisfied with it. It is not quite all-embracing enough. So he equally expertly selects a second general statement, from Leviticus 19:18, which requires also love for one's neighbour, a love that is on a par with our own self-respect. Religion for Jesus is all about responses and relationships, both to God and to others.

It has sometimes been questioned as to whether 'Thou shalt love' is not a contradiction in terms. Is love something that can be commanded? We may argue, 'No! Love is an emotion. It's either there or it isn't. Who would want to be the victim of a love that was commanded?' But this is the teaching of Jesus, and we can't just dismiss it like that. Surely he must have meant something more than an emotion. And the clue is in the four words 'heart, soul, mind, strength'. Love involves the whole personality – intelligence and will, as well as emotions. Love is not a passive thing. It involves the use of all our strength, all our will.

It has been said that, while both commands were known to Jesus' hearers, the new thing in what he said here was to link 'Love your god' with 'Love your neighbour'. Again, this does not mean just that we should 'like our neighbour'. Liking is emotional and variable, and often those around us are not likeable, but they are always lovable. We must hate the sin, but still love the sinner.

Lordship in the Kingdom

'While the Pharisees were gathered together, Jesus asked them,
"What do you think about the Christ? Whose son is he?" . . . He said
to them, "How is it then that David . . . calls him 'Lord'? . . . How
can he be his son?" ' (vv. 41–43).

Jesus was telling the Pharisees that even if they went as far as the crowd in accepting him as Messiah in the sense of 'son of David', they would not be going far enough. They needed to accept him as Messiah in the sense of 'Lord', 'Son of God'. If people were going to call him Messiah, they must realise the full meaning of the term. Likewise, if we wish to be members of the kingdom we must accept the Lordship of Christ in his kingdom.

This is surely to say that the origins of the kingdom are not just human, but divine. The ministry of Jesus is not to be seen as an event in history, the logical outcome of the development of Jewish life and history, though it is both of those. It is to be seen as an intervention by God through his Son, his express image. 'The kingdom of the world has become the kingdom of our Lord and of his Christ, and he will reign for ever and ever' (Revelation 11:15). (Again, the 'Lord' here refers to God the Father, not Jesus.)

The kingdom of which Jesus so frequently speaks is God's kingdom and Jesus is the Christ, God's Anointed One, appointed to rule God's kingdom. And Messiahship is not to be seen in terms of nationalistic, political or military terms of power and glory.

It is because it is Jesus who 'will reign for ever and ever' that the kingdom is as it is. The nature of the kingdom stems from the nature of the King. We can be as religious as the Pharisees, and still be in the stern and relentless kind of legal righteousness, or ascendancy for our own religious prejudices.

But the kingdom of Jesus is the kingdom of God, and that is a different thing altogether, as Jesus was continually pointing out. He is not just a 'second David', but Son of the living God. It is only when we share his nature that we are citizens of his kingdom.

Excuses! Excuses! (2)

'They all alike began to make excuses' (v. 18).

The First Excuse was: 'I have just bought a field, and I must go and see it. Please excuse me' (v. 18). A twenty-first-century, Western cultural equivalent of this excuse could be: 'I've purchased a holiday house over the mobile phone and must go and inspect the structure of the building and where it's located.'

Hardly a plausible excuse! In first-century Palestine no one purchased a field without knowing every square metre of the land. Buying and selling was and still is today a long and demanding business.

The Second Excuse was: 'I have just bought five yoke of oxen, and I'm on my way to try them out. Please excuse me' (v. 19). A twenty-first-century, Western cultural equivalent of this excuse could be: 'I've just purchased five used cars by SMS on my mobile phone and I'm now on my way to find out the models and the condition of the vehicles.'

Another unbelievable excuse! In first-century Palestine teams of oxen were taken to the marketplace where a small field was available for prospective buyers to test the oxen before purchase.

The Third Excuse was: 'I have just got married, so I can't come' (v. 20). In first-century Palestine, had there been a wedding in the village the host of the feast would have rescheduled his feast, for no Middle Eastern village could afford the luxury of having two grand events on the same day.

The host's response to these three excuses was not one of retaliation in anger but of grace. He sent his servant to invite the poor, the marginalised and the outcast of the village.

A constant temptation for disciples of the early twenty-first century is to become preoccupied with material possessions, business matters and domestic ties. These are among the many subtle snares that can make the disciple deaf to the claims and priority of Jesus Christ and his mission.

More Portraits of Christ

Colonel Henry Gariepy's book, 100 Portraits of Christ, *is a collection of names and titles ascribed to Jesus in Scripture. They reveal the person and ministry of Christ. The book, published on behalf of The Salvation Army by Scripture Press Publications Inc, USA, in 1987, is now out of print.*

Introduction

Names and titles of Jesus revealed in the Bible were given by God to honour Christ and to give us a clearer understanding of who he is. They give us a better grasp of his power, glory and greatness. Each is a revealing portrait of our Lord, providing fresh insights and applications of their meaning for Christian living.

These brief studies of further names and titles given to Jesus will lead us to know our Lord better and to follow him more faithfully in our daily Christian life.

God

'Thomas said to him, "My Lord and my God!"' (John 20:28).

The divinity of Jesus Christ is the cornerstone of Christian theology, attested by Scripture. Paul writes of Christ: 'Who, being in very nature God' (v. 6). The word for nature in the Greek text is *morphe*. It is a Greek philosophical term meaning 'shape'; but also more than that, it permanently identifies Christ with the nature and character of God. The word denotes that the essential nature of divinity comes from within and is permanently a part of him.

By contrast, Paul also states (v. 8) that Christ was found in appearance as a human being. The Greek word for appearance is *schema* and denotes that which is assumed from the outside and does not come from within the essential nature. Our Lord's divinity came from his inmost and essential nature whereas his humanness was assumed from the outside.

John, who had the most intimate contact with Christ, declared that in Christ the 'Word was God' (John 1:1). Thomas, who was a follower with a practical turn of mind, on seeing the risen Christ testified, 'My Lord and my God.'

Paul states: 'For in Christ all the fulness of the deity lives in bodily form' (Colossians 2:9), while in writing to Titus he says, 'We wait for the . . . glorious appearing of our great God and Saviour, Jesus Christ' (2:13).

The history of the Church attests to the divinity of Jesus, while this is also corroborated by personal experience. A newly converted man was chided at work: 'Now don't tell me that you believe that story about Jesus turning water into wine!' – to which the new convert replied, 'I don't know about that, but in my house he certainly turned beer into furniture!' Countless lives testify of a total transformation, an inward power and peace that results from the divine work of the risen and reigning Christ.

Prayer

Divine Christ, save me from a limited concept of you. Help me to think and believe big enough, and to avoid the pitfall of a myopic faith.

Christ

' "We have found the Messiah" (that is, the Christ)' (v. 41).

Christ is the Greek equivalent of the Hebrew 'Messiah'. It means the 'Anointed One'. This title was especially associated with prophecy. Messiah is the Seed of the Woman in Genesis; the Star and Sceptre in Numbers; the Redeemer in Job; the Rose of Sharon in the Song of Solomon; the Lord of Righteousness in Jeremiah, and so on.

Messiah was prophesied to come, and many aspects of his coming – the city of his birth; John the Baptist's work; his sojourn in Egypt; his type of ministry; his betrayal, death and resurrection – were all foretold in details that only Christ could fulfil.

At the time Jesus was born, there was an air of expectancy that the Messiah would come. Thus the statement of the Samaritan woman: ' "I know that Messiah" (called Christ) "is coming" ' (John 4:25). Thus the elated announcement by Andrew to his brother Peter: 'We have found the Messiah' (1:41). The Sanhedrin demanded of him, 'If you are the Christ . . . tell us' (Luke 22:67).

The story is told of a woman who lived alone in the hills of America's South and had all along her living-room walls pictures of Robert E. Lee. One night in a snowstorm two men came to her house for temporary shelter. When leaving, one of them, distinguished in appearance, gave her a little gift. The woman asked the other man the name of her kind guest. He replied, 'That, ma'am, is General Robert E. Lee.' Though she had his pictures, she did not recognise him when he came.

The Messiah was portrayed in the Old Testament and these prophecies were known to every devout Jew. Yet most did not recognise and accept him as the Messiah when he came. Their concept was too materialistic or nationalistic instead of spiritual.

Prayer

Christ, fulfil your great and gracious purposes in my life. Help me to recognise where you are in every situation.

Teacher

'We know you are a teacher who has come from God' (v. 2).

The Gospels are full of references to Jesus' teaching ministry. It is commonly reported that 'Jesus went throughout Galilee, teaching in their synagogues' (Matthew 4:23). On the mountainside, Jesus taught his disciples and gave the world the 'Sermon on the Mount' (Matthew 5–7). But he also taught 'one-on-one'. He taught Nicodemus the mystery and meaning of the new birth. Nicodemus, a teacher himself, acknowledged the more-than-human quality of Jesus' teaching as he said, 'We know you are a teacher who has come from God' (John 3:2).

At the other end of the social spectrum, we find him giving his great dissertation on worship and living water to *one* woman. In doing so he not only crossed the boundary of respectability by conversing with a woman of unsavoury character, but also of the racial polarisation that existed between Jews and Samaritans. The school of Christ is without walls and boundaries of any kind.

The impact on the hearers of Jesus' teaching was amazement at his wisdom and utterances. We find them exclaiming, 'Where *did* this man get these things?' (Mark 6:2). On another occasion, we read: 'The crowds were amazed at his teaching, because he taught them as one who had authority' (Matthew 7:28, 29). When our Lord was arrested in the Garden of Gethsemane, he chided the mob: 'Every day I sat in the temple courts teaching, and you did not arrest me' (Matthew 26:55).

As teacher, he had none of the resources we have today – amplification, visuals, media, electronic aids. Yet, what he taught has never become outdated but is as timely and timeless as when his words resonated throughout Galilee.

One of the great privileges of our Christian experience is to have the teachings of Jesus as recorded in the Gospels for our enlightenment and enrichment. May we who know him as our Saviour and Lord also know him as our teacher. What incredible truths he has to share with us! 'Teach me your way, O LORD, and I will walk in your truth' (Psalm 86:11).

Carpenter

'Isn't this the carpenter?' (v. 3).

The New Testament word for carpenter, *tekton*, means an artisan, a craftsman, or one who is a builder. The cosmic Carpenter by the miracle of incarnation became the carpenter of Nazareth. But this question asked in Nazareth is the only window in the Scriptures through which we may look on the years of his young manhood.

The absence of Joseph from the later Gospel narratives seems to suggest that he had died and Jesus, the elder brother, took over the support of the family until the other brothers were old enough.

G. A. Studdert Kennedy has framed this portrait of our Lord in memorable verse, entitled 'The Carpenter':

> I wonder what he charged for chairs at Nazareth?
> And did men try to beat him down
> And boast about it in the town –
> 'I bought it cheap for half-a-crown
> From that mad carpenter'?
>
> I wonder did he have bad debts,
> And did he know my fears and frets?
> The Gospel writer here forgets
> To tell about the Carpenter.

This portrait of Christ as a carpenter identifies him with mankind. How reassuring to know that he who now holds a sceptre in his hand once held a hammer and a saw! As he worked day after day, smoothing yokes for oxen, making the wood obedient to his skill, his hands would become roughened, the kind of hands strong fishermen would look at and know that they could follow him with confidence and respect. He knows the meaning of toil. He understands our burdens, our weariness, our tasks.

Today the carpenter of Nazareth who once smoothed yokes in his skilful hands will take a *life* that is yielded to him and fashion it into a beautiful and useful instrument of God's eternal kingdom.

Servant

'Here is my servant . . . my chosen one' (v. 1).

Imagine, the Sovereign of the universe – a servant! What a peerless paradox! From what exalted heights to what unspeakable depths the Lord of the universe came to be the Saviour of mankind! The Gospel narrator in Matthew 12:18 quotes the word of God to the prophet Isaiah as being fulfilled in Christ: Christ came to be a servant; he came to give his life for us.

In the Gospels we never find him pursuing his own interests. His whole life and ministry was for others. Paul, contemplating the marvel and majesty of this sublime truth, expressed it in immortal words: '[He] made himself nothing, taking the very nature of a servant . . . he humbled himself and became obedient to death – even death on a cross!' (Philippians 2:7–8).

When some of the disciples displayed ambition for position and promotion, our Lord set down the rules of what Christian living is all about: 'Whoever wants to become great among you must be your servant . . . just as the Son of Man did not come to be served, but to serve, and to give his life as a ransom for many' (Matthew 20:26–28).

These are hard words in a world that seems obsessed with pleasure, possessions, perquisites and success. But servanthood becomes the terms of discipleship. We are all called to be servants of our Lord. But it is a servanthood of the highest privilege and profession.

Colonel James Irwin, a former astronaut, shares that while walking on the moon he realised that when he would return to Earth many would consider him an international celebrity. Realising his role as a Christian, he records: 'As I was returning to Earth, I realised that I was a servant, not a celebrity. I am here as God's servant to share what I have experienced that others might know the glory of God.'

If Christ, Lord of the universe, became a servant for us, can we do any less for him?

———————

Prayer

Dear Lord, my model for living, help me by your grace, not to seek to be served, but to serve.

78

Friend

'And they say, "Here is . . . a friend"' (v. 19).

'Every man passes his life in search for friendship,' wrote Emerson. Henry Ford once described 'your best friend' as the one who 'helps you bring out of yourself the best that is in you'. And Helen Parker wrote in her poem, 'Discovery':

> Today a man discovered gold and fame;
> Another flew the stormy seas;
> Another saw an unnamed world aflame;
> One found the germ of a disease.
> But what high fates my paths attend:
> For I – today I found a friend.

Jesus gave the supreme test of friendship when he said, 'Greater love has no-one than this, that he lay down his life for his friends' (John 15:13).

During the First World War, a soldier saw his friend wounded out in no-man's land. The man asked his officer, 'May I go, Sir, and bring him in?' The officer refused, saying, 'No, if you go I will only lose you as well.' Disobeying the officer, the man went for his friend. Somehow, he managed to get him on his shoulder and stagger back to his trench, only to fall mortally wounded himself. The officer was angry: 'I told you not to go. Now I have lost two good men. It was not worth it!' With his dying breath, the man said, 'But it was worth it, Sir, because when I got to him he said, "Jim, I knew you'd come."'

Our best friend is the One who laid down his life for us. He went out to no-man's land, and himself was mortally wounded as he rescued us from the destruction of sin. He wants to be our friend and has given us the condition of his friendship: 'You are my friends if you do what I command' (John 15:14). But his commandments are not burdens; they are life and liberty to the soul. Jesus, the greatest lover of our soul, leans out of his immensity to say, 'My friend.' He waits for our response: 'My Lord and God.' Then will we know his transforming friendship.

Sell All

*'I consider everything a loss compared to the surpassing
greatness of knowing Christ Jesus' (Philippians 3:8).*

The story Jesus told about the hidden treasure in the field was not an
improbable occurrence in first-century Palestine. The burying of
treasure in the fields of Palestine occurred so often that many similar
stories circulated in conversation. In the Middle East the pearl was
considered supremely precious. In the first century, divers fished for pearls
in waters from the Red Sea to the Persian Gulf to the Indian Ocean. Such
was the demand for pearls that exceptionally large amounts of money were
paid in India, Mesopotamia and Persia.

Consider an overview of the twin parables of the hidden treasure and
the costly pearl:

* Both have two features in common, the idea of finding something
highly valuable and the thought of selling everything to obtain it.
* In both parables the discovery is a surprise, which results in joy.
There is the overwhelming experience of the wonder and joy of their
discovery.

The decisive thing in the parables is not what the two men surrender, but
their joy in discovering the pearl. Is this not also true when we discover
Jesus, 'the pearl of great price'? The effect of the discovery is overwhelming
and overpowering. It fills the heart with joy and gladness and produces the
most wholehearted self-surrender and sacrifice of self and one's
possessions.

The twentieth-century Scottish theologian P. T. Forsyth wrote: 'I should
count a life well spent and the world well lost if, after tasting all its
experiences and facing all its problems, I had not more to show at its close,
or carry with me to another life, than the acquisition of a real, sure, humble
and grateful faith in the eternal and incarnate Son of God.'[1]

Advocate

'If anyone sins, we have an advocate with the Father,
Jesus Christ the righteous' (v. 1, NKJV).

The word 'advocate' here is the Greek word *parakletos* which John's Gospel also uses in chapters 14 to 16 as a term for the Holy Spirit. However, here the word is applied to Jesus himself. The word means 'one called alongside to help, one to plead our cause'.

The Holy Spirit as Paraclete can do many things for us. He convicts, regenerates or brings about the new birth, empowers, guides, purifies, helps us in our praying. But there is one thing the Holy Spirit cannot do for us. He cannot acquit us from our guilt of sin. Jesus Christ alone can be our advocate, our Paraclete, in achieving our pardon in the divine court of justice.

In the time when this Scripture was written, the word translated 'advocate' referred to one who took one's side in a trial. There is a divine law that has been broken. God's law declares: 'The soul that sinneth, it shall die' (Ezekiel 18:20, *KJV*). We have all sinned and come under the condemnation of that law. We are guilty. We are under the death sentence. Who can help us?

We have an advocate – one who pleads our cause. He intercedes on our behalf. Not to prove our innocence, for we are guilty. We have grieved him by a thousand falls, but we have an advocate who stands on our behalf at the bar of divine justice.

- *Jesus* (his human name as part of today's text) reminds us of his understanding of our frailties and failures.
- *Christ* reminds us he is God's Anointed, having a unique standing with God the Father and will have the attention of the divine judge.
- *The righteous* reminds us he has the moral qualifications fitting him to be the mediator between man and God.

Prayer

My advocate with the Father, thank you for pleading my cause. By the merit of your sacrifice, may I have pardon, and by the cleansing of your Spirit, may I have purity.

Saviour

'This is indeed the Christ, Saviour of the world' (John 4:42, NKJV).

This title was not new to the ancient world. Egyptian kings and Roman emperors were often called saviours. But Jesus took this title and gave it new and eternal meaning.

In the New Testament this title is found most in 2 Peter, where it is used five times. Peter knew Christ well as Saviour, as when he started to walk out on the waves and cried desperately for Christ to save him. But there were other tempests within, from which Peter was rescued by Christ – when he was prone to base denial and faithlessness.

At a World Congress on Evangelism, delegates were deeply moved by the testimony of Kimo, one of the Auca killers of missionaries some years previously in the jungle of interior Ecuador. When asked in an interview what Jesus had done to change his life, he replied, 'I don't live the same way I did before, I don't live sinning now. Now I live speaking to God.'

What a classic example of Christ's mighty salvation in modern times! Others in history have been called 'saviour' but Christ alone is able to measure up to the full meaning of this title.

I know a soul that is steeped in sin,
That no man's art can cure;
But I know a Name, a Name, a Name,
That can make that soul all pure.

I know a life that is lost to God,
Bound down by things of earth;
But I know a Name, a Name, a Name,
That can bring that soul new birth.

I know of lands that are sunk in shame,
Of hearts that faint and tire;
But I know a Name, a Name, a Name,
That will set those lands on fire.

(Anon)

Atoning Sacrifice

*'He is the atoning sacrifice for our sins, and not only for ours
but also for the sins of the whole world' (v. 2).*

Christ is 'the atoning sacrifice for our sins', declares the person who
knew him better than any other human being. The word 'atoning' is
variously translated: 'propitiation', 'expiation', 'atonement', 'remedy',
'sacrifice'. Each word eloquently testifies to the supreme sacrifice Jesus
made on the cross for each of us.

His was a voluntary offering for us. It was the world's supreme act of
self-giving and had the greatest impact of any event of history. His death
set a gallows against every city skyline and redeemed a world from sin.

Atonement, simply defined as 'making at-one-ment' or uniting that
which was separated, is the purpose of Christ having come to earth. His
birth, life, death, resurrection and coming again are all summed up in this
theological term. This mission of Christ is imaginatively expressed by
Major Albert Hambleton:

> He didn't come to Jupiter,
> He didn't come to Mars,
> He didn't come to sun or moon
> Or any of the stars.
> Of all the vast created host
> From his own hand unfurled
> By Jesus Christ, his only Son,
> God came into our world.
> He came because he wanted most
> To take away sin's blight:
> To frustrate every devilish scheme
> And put our wrong world right.
> His own volition brought him from
> His throne with splendor pearled.
> But only if invited will
> He come into my world.

Our Hope

'Christ Jesus our hope' (1 Timothy 1:1).

'Hopeless' is one of the saddest words of the English language. Hopelessness impinges on us every day from the media and from our own encounters with life. An illness, without hope of recovery; a departure, without hope of return; a mountain avalanche, without hope of rescue; a child lost, without hope of being found.

Mankind was lost in sin. He could do nothing to save himself. He was helpless – but not hopeless. As hymnwriter William Hawley writes:

> A light came out of darkness;
> No light, no hope had we,
> Till Jesus came from heaven
> Our light and hope to be.
> (*SASB* 94)

In his epistles Paul writes of 'Christ in you, the hope of glory' (Colossians 1:27). In his letter to Titus he refers to the return of our Lord as 'the blessed hope' (2:13). We need never despair – Christ is our hope. And Hebrews 6:19 assures us that Christ is sufficient for all the storms and stresses of life for 'we have this hope as an anchor for the soul, firm and secure'.

How precious is this hope when we say a final goodbye to loved ones! We do not 'grieve like the rest of men, who have no hope. We believe that Jesus died and rose again and so we believe that God will bring with Jesus those who have fallen asleep in him' (1 Thessalonians 4:13–14).

Our songs of faith pulsate with the hope we have in Christ. With R. H. McDaniel we affirm, 'I'm possessed of a hope that is steadfast and sure, since Jesus came into my heart' (*SASB* 394). And with Bernard of Clairvaux we affirm that Christ is the 'hope of every contrite heart' (*SASB* 61).

Prayer

Dear Lord, thank you for the sure and certain hope we have in you, for the needs of this life and for life to come.

Head

'Speaking the truth in love, we will in all things grow up into him who is the Head, that is, Christ' (v. 15).

Paul was calling the Christians at Ephesus to maturity in Christ (v. 13). He goes on to say that we are not to remain in spiritual infancy, unstable and gullible, but committed to the truth and 'in all things [to] grow up into him who is the Head, that is, Christ' (v. 15).

Maturity and the headship of Christ are intertwined in the Christian life. When we try to lead our own lives and do not acknowledge his authority, we live in spiritual immaturity. It is only when Christ is our head, our leader, our authority, that we grow to maturity in him. There is no growth apart from him.

The title 'Head' denotes pre-eminence. Christ must be our Sovereign as well as our Saviour. Augustine summarised it: 'Christ is not valued at all unless he be valued above all.' Albert Schweitzer called Christ 'an imperious ruler' and went on to say that as we obey his commands we come to know the enrichment and strengthening of his fellowship.

There are some who have authority by conferment – it comes to them from without. They may or may not measure up to the trust and responsibility of the power vested in them.

Others have authority by virtue of their character and leadership, with or without the conferred status. They have respect and a following because of who and what they are. With these few people along life's road, it is not a burden but a privilege to serve under their leadership. Their wisdom, integrity, fairness, sensitivity, and love make it a joy to follow them and be under their leading.

Jesus Christ is our head, with both conferred authority as the Son of God and earned authority for his infinite love and goodness.

The highest privilege of service is under the headship, the divine authority of Jesus Christ. When we have the Lord as our head, then there is symmetry, harmony, and efficient function. May we know him as our living head – our leader and ultimate authority.

The Amen

'These are the words of the Amen' (v. 14).

'Amen' is one of the great Bible words. It means 'so be it'. It also affirms that what it relates to is trustworthy and sure.

We read: 'Then all the people shall say, "Amen!"' no less than twelve consecutive times in Deuteronomy 27:15–26. They were saying, 'So be it' in response to the reciting by the Levites of curses on sins. The Psalms use the word as a conclusion to praise, such as 'Praise be to the LORD for ever! Amen and Amen' (89:52).

In the New Testament, it accompanies expressions of praise and prayer, such as in Paul's doxology in Romans 11:33–36, which ends, 'To him be the glory for ever! Amen.'

But the word has its greatest association with our Lord, occurring more than 100 times in the Gospels. Translated 'verily', it is always doubled in John – 'Verily, verily I say unto you' (*KJV*). Wherever Jesus uses this expression, he is giving special emphasis to a vital truth. We need to heed most carefully the 'verilies' of Christ. The *New International Version* translates it as 'I tell you the truth'. Jesus said to Nicodemus, 'I tell you the truth, no-one can enter the kingdom of God unless he is born of water and the Spirit' (John 3:5). This word intensifies the truth that new birth is the invariable requisite for all mankind.

With such a close association of this word, and investing it with the authority of his person and teaching, it is not surprising that in the final book it becomes a title for Christ himself. Christ ascribes the title to himself in the last of the seven letters to the churches and just before the magnificent vision of the throne and end times that is given to John. It is Christ's own seal of the trustworthiness and the surety of the stupendous revelation of this book, as he declares, 'These are the words of the Amen' (Revelation 3:14).

It is significant that this word 'Amen' is universally the same so that Christians of all nations and languages, when they come together, unitedly praise God as all the people say, 'Amen!'

Small Beginnings (1):

The Mustard Seed

'The smallest seed you plant in the ground . . . grows and becomes the largest of all garden plants' (vv. 31, 32).

Michael Zohary, an Israeli botanist, notes that the mustard seed is very small, the size of a pinhead, yet grows into a small tree of some ten feet in height where birds nest and feed on the abundance of its small black seeds.

The birds roosting in the branches of the tree (v. 32) are symbolic in the Old Testament for the nations (see Ezekiel 17:23, 31:6; Daniel 4:12, 21). The kingdom will be universal; people of all nations will be found in it.

The importance of this parable is seen in that it is recorded in all three Synoptic Gospels. In Matthew and Luke it is recorded alongside the parable of the leaven. In the Old Testament, unlike the leaven, the mustard seed is not mentioned. Instead, the picture of the large cedar tree was common in Judaism to describe the kingdom, and the image is a consistent one to be found in the Old Testament (see Ezekiel 17:22–24).

The cedar tree is also frequently used as a symbol of strength, so the use by Jesus of a mustard seed to describe the kingdom of God is a totally unexpected surprise.

As with so many of his parables, Jesus does not follow the accepted religious or cultural script of his day. Here is yet another one of those twists in the story that takes his audience by complete surprise. Likening the coming kingdom of God to, of all things, a tiny insignificant mustard seed as against the mighty cedar seed and subsequent tree, was almost insulting the majesty and power of God's kingdom to the Jewish mind.

Jesus teaches that the kingdom of God comes in an unexpected and surprising form. Jesus himself is the kingdom of God – *autobasileia* is the Greek word – and he comes in the form of the lowly, humble servant of God to die on a Roman cross used for the worst of criminals.

The Cup

A series by Major Beverly Ivany

Introduction

In this brief series, we look at a simple cup and visualise it as a symbol of life. It can represent our inner spiritual journey, and we can learn things from it. Whatever the cup holds eventually must be emptied out, in order to receive once again. We always need to make room for the new. For it is a natural rhythm of life – emptying and filling; giving and receiving; accepting and letting go.

As we read each day, perhaps we can do so with a cup of coffee or tea close by – in order to look at the cup. As we observe it, then internalise what the words are saying to us, may we sense God's presence in a powerful way.

Major Beverly Ivany is a Salvation Army officer in Canada, where she has served with her husband David. In their early years of service together they were corps officers (church ministers); they later became divisional leaders and then Beverly was involved in overseeing the process for people applying to be Salvation Army officers throughout the Canada and Bermuda Territory. They have four children.

Beverly is to be the next writer of Words of Life, *her first issue being the January–April 2012 edition. She has degrees in English and music, her Masters in theological studies, and is the author of two books for young people.*

The Cup of Life

'And if anyone gives even a cup of cold water to one of these little ones because he is my disciple, I tell you the truth, he will certainly not lose his reward' (v. 42).

The cup of cold water, referred to by Jesus, has come to symbolise the cup of life to many. It represents sustenance and vitality, bringing a sense of hope for the one who drinks from it. For each of us, this cup can also represent our spiritual life and journey with Christ.

It's wonderful to enjoy a good cup of coffee or tea! They are drinks that bring both refreshment and certain relaxation. It's anticipated daily, often leading into good conversations with others. We often use the same cup when at home, or at work. It's a familiar cup, and often not all that fancy. It might even have stains, and might not be new. But it's ours. Take a look at the cup: sides, a bottom, an open top. It's functional, ready to receive the drink.

Our lives are like the cup in so many ways. Ordinary, yet very special. It is filled, then emptied – something like the rhythm of breathing; in, and out. The cup sometimes becomes stained. But it can soon be washed, becoming clean again; for God's forgiveness cleanses and makes us whiter than snow. There are boundaries, like the sides and bottom; yet we are to be open, willing to receive all God has for us. As we continue to thirst for him, he is always there; to infill us with his love, and his grace.

Our special cup, our unique personality, is one-of-a-kind. God desires to dance his way into our life, into our innermost being. It's a mystery, to be indwelt by God Almighty. Yet we know it to be a reality. For he desires to fill us daily, afresh, with his boundless love and goodness.

The cup, our relationship with Christ, then with others – this is what life is all about. What glory is ours when filled by the Lord!

Prayer

Father, I pray you will pour your abundant love into my cup, into the veins of my soul. I am yours. Fill me afresh today.

Emptying the Cup

'Who, being in very nature God, did not consider equality with God something to be grasped, but made himself nothing' (vv. 6–7).

The spiritual journey is one of repeatedly emptying, then filling. It is the emptying that is the difficult part for most. But it can also be rewarding and fulfilling in many ways – similar to drinking from a cup, which brings certain joy and satisfaction.

Of course, the experience depends upon what is in the cup. Sometimes the cup is filled with a drink that isn't good. Water that is contaminated; or milk that has gone sour. It could be as simple as a hot drink, gone cold. No matter, the process is the same. For it is a cycle; the emptying must come, before the filling.

What is in our lives that needs to be emptied out, in order to receive? Perhaps it is sin – secret, hidden sins – causing stains that are tough to remove. It could be merely complacency, which can be damaging and detrimental for receiving anything good and wholesome. We can only be filled with God's Spirit if we clear out all that is not of him.

There are no doubt very good things in our lives as well. Things that are positive in the cup of life. Yet it's crucial to give these same things over to God; to not hold on to them for our own sakes. Rather, to allow ourselves to be completely free – empty, open, vulnerable before God – in order to be filled again and again with his grace.

The rhythm of life is essential for our cups, our lives, to be of worth to our heavenly Father. The emptying, then the filling. Daily breathing in the very breath of God, over and over. It comes down to trusting God with who we are; believing, as he ministers to us, that we will have joy and inner peace – enabling us to reach out to others in need; to help them realise the great potential in their cup of life, as they seek Christ and his amazing love.

May today be a day of refreshment. May it be a day when we empty all, realising our nothingness before God; then be ready for, and receptive to, his glorious infilling of abundant love.

The Chipped Cup

*'How can you say to your brother, "Let me take the speck out of your eye,"
when all the time there is a plank in your own eye?' (v. 4).*

Sometimes in life we simply want familiar things around us, to make us feel at ease. When we have a morning cup of coffee or tea, we often gravitate to our favourite cup – even if it's flawed or chipped. It doesn't really matter. In a funny way, it's the comfort of it that counts. It's the sentimentality of the known.

We don't think through the obvious, that the chipped cup could cause a cut to the lip; or the certain crack in the cup, due to age, could be dangerous. We still hold on to it, for some reason. We've become accustomed to the flaw. We seldom even notice it.

As for ourselves, there are no doubt certain imperfections and flaws in our character, for we are not perfect people. It could be a problem of attitude; or a certain chip on our shoulder. All of us fall so short from what God wants us to be, what he truly wants from us as his children. We have our inadequacies and our shortcomings, which hold us back from living up to our potential in Christ. So, what can we do, and how can we change?

Our desire, our longing, is to be more like Christ. The chips and cracks in our lives make us realise how we need to be remoulded, reshaped, cleaned out – in order to receive all he has for us. These same chips help us to understand others better; to have an empathetic heart, in order to help them work through the various issues in their lives.

We must always be careful that we do not use our flaws as excuses. Our imperfections are to be brought before Christ, for a complete cleansing. Our chipped cup needs to be fixed and made right again; the grime needs to be washed and removed, in order to shine brighter for the Lord.

It is then, and only then, that we can present our life to him, in all honesty and integrity. For suddenly, the cup of our life will sparkle, and be inviting for others to explore the possibility of eternal life with Christ. For it will be a cup fit for a King!

The Paper Cup

*'I am the LORD your God . . . Open wide your mouth
and I will fill it' (v. 10).*

Life is often fragile. It is something like a paper cup, which isn't sturdy; also, it's somewhat unsteady. Yet it still does the job; for it has sides, a bottom and an open top. For the most part, we are not nearly as comfortable with a paper cup. Neither is it cherished like other cups, for there is no attachment to it. In fact it's usually thrown away at the end of the drink, for it has served its purpose. It's usually rather drab and unappealing in appearance.

Sometimes we might feel something like that paper cup – used, unattractive, lifeless. We might be put in situations where we find ourselves feeling rather useless, drained, exhausted, tired from all we do. We become sapped of any energy we might have once had – having given to others, over and over again. We might even feel rather vulnerable, fragile.

It's then that God speaks. He reminds us that we *are* truly valued. He might even remind us of one of his creations, the beautiful butterflies – needing to spread their wings each morning, to receive sunshine from above. Why? Because the scales on their wings are solar. Without the source of energy from the sun, they cannot fly.

Oh yes, how we need to fly! How we need to receive from the Source! For when we do, we receive his divine energy. He takes our paper-cup lives and fills them with his grace, his mercy, his unfathomable love. The Lord affirms that we are of such great worth. He brings strength, nourishment, refreshment. He makes us strong, and firm in our faith. And then he whispers in our ears that we are truly beautiful in his sight.

———————

Thought

Sometime today, have a drink out of a paper cup. Feel its fragility, noting that it is probably quite plain and not particularly attractive. As you hold it, pray for those who feel vulnerable, the marginalised in society – that they will sense God's presence today, like never before.

Cup of Sorrow

*'My Father, if it is possible, may this cup be taken from me.
Yet not as I will, but as you will' (v. 39).*

We all experience sorrow, at some time or another. Pain is so difficult, whether it be physical, emotional, spiritual; whether it be ours or the pain of someone close to us. We never thought it could penetrate so deeply into our being, our psyche. We cry out in desperation – yet often we feel God does not hear; we don't know what to do, where to go with it all. We feel so alone, so abandoned, so isolated. Where are you, God?

'Eloi, Eloi, lama sabachthani?' – which means, 'My God, my God, why have you forsaken me?' (Matthew 27:46).

Some people seem to be afflicted with pain and agony, far more than others. You know them. The cup of sorrow seems to be constantly filled. Someone like Job, who loved God supremely. A man of integrity; one who was so faithful – even through his deep pain. Yet, after all he went through, he finally heard the voice of God speak directly to him. He knew he was loved by God, and that God was with him. Ultimately, that's all that mattered to Job.

Jesus was suffering, and knew that more anguish was in store for him. When he was finally hung on that bitter cross to die, all he really wanted was God's presence; to know that the Father was with him and had not abandoned him. He drank that ultimate cup of sorrow for you and for me. We wouldn't be here today, with the promised hope of eternal life, if it were not for that cup.

As we contemplate our lives and the lives of those near and dear to us, may we remember that Christ is always with us. He will never leave us, nor forsake us; for we are his precious children. May we reach out, in a practical way, to someone going through a difficult time right now: a phone call; a letter; a visit. May we bring to them a sense of God's divine presence, comfort and assurance.

The Cup Overflowing

'You anoint my head with oil; my cup overflows' (v. 5).

The cup of blessing is a term which comes from the Jewish Passover rite. Yes, the cup is blessed; but the cup itself holds a blessing – which is the gift of life. And not only one blessing, but many blessings. The cup overflows.

What is a blessing? One dictionary defines that it is to consecrate or *hallow* by a religious rite or words; to pronounce something holy or sacred. It's not really making something sacred, but rather acknowledging the sacredness contained already.

Again, in the Hebrew Scriptures, a blessing is something which communicates divine life. Blessings, or *berakahs*, were often shared, according to Jewish tradition. They were given to bring happiness, to encourage, to invoke divine care, to thank others, to keep safe. For whenever God chooses to bless us, bounteous life emerges and indeed erupts. Goodness abounds.

Anyone and anything that brings something of God into our cup of life is a blessing; for blessings say to us that God is present. It's important to note that sometimes blessings come in disguise; through pain and sorrow, through discouragement and disappointment, through hardship and extreme frustration. Yet we can look back and mysteriously see how God turns deep sorrow, disappointment and hardship into such joy. A cup overflowing.

It's then we are able to come out of ourselves and turn to others. The blessing expands. The gift of life is shared with another. For God's love is indeed like having a bottomless cup. The more we drink from his abundance, the more love there always seems to be to receive from him and to give to those who are thirsty for his grace. Indeed, showers of blessing!

Today, may we take in and treasure all the blessings he has for us. May we never take any of them for granted. May we always verbally thank him for the cup of life – overflowing with all he has for us. And as we radiate his beauty in our lives, may we bring a blessing to each person we encounter, with whom we share life.

Small Beginnings (2):

The Leaven

'It is like yeast that a woman took and mixed into a large amount of flour until it worked all through the dough' (v. 21).

In first-century Palestine, bread was the staple food and was made from wheat or, in the case of the poor, from barley. As a child Jesus would have often observed his mother, Mary, taking the wheat or barley flour in the evening, adding water and a pinch of salt, mixing the small piece of leaven into the batch of flour and then covering the mixed dough with a cloth to stand overnight.

Early next morning, Jesus with his mother would find that the whole mass of dough was leavened. It was now a bubbling, heaving mixture, fermented and ready for placing into the small oven to bake the family's daily supply of bread.

Most modern translations of the New Testament obscure the real meaning of leaven by translating the Greek word *zume*, not as leaven but as yeast. In the ancient world, yeast (as we know it, as being fresh, clean and wholesome) was not commonly available. The much less wholesome leaven had to be used. By keeping back a piece of the previous week's dough, juices were added to the piece of dough, which promoted the process of fermentation from which the leaven was produced.

In this parable Jesus uses the leaven to teach the hidden dynamic power and influence of its fermentation effect upon the batch of dough. He teaches that when the reign of God invades human history nothing can be unaffected by it. We can be sure that the fermenting dynamic impact of the reign of God has begun and is continuing.

There was in our Lord's ministry no element of external coercion, but in it, as theologian C. H. Dodd commented, 'the power of God's kingdom worked from within, mightily permeating the dead lump of religious Judaism in his time'.[2]

God Has Come for Our Salvation

A series for Advent by

Lieutenant-Colonel André Sterckx

Introduction

'Christmas can be every day for you' is the title of one of the many songs written by Major Joy Webb OF (Order of the Founder). It could be an apt introduction to the Advent series that I have prepared. I firmly believe that when God acts in our lives, heaven not only opens but also reaches into life around us – as stories of Bible heroes show.

Heaven is very near, however dark situations can be. It brings light in the soul today and illuminates each tomorrow. Then we can communicate the angels' message: the glorious God has come in power for our salvation, resulting in total peace for all.

Belgian-born, but French and Swiss citizen alike, André Sterckx is a son of Salvation Army officers. After a time in teaching, André himself became an officer in 1958. Service in Belgium and Switzerland saw him involved in pastoral ministry, then teaching, training, editorial and administration appointments. He later headed up The Salvation Army in Italy as Officer Commanding before returning to Switzerland to be Training Principal of the Army's South-European training college in Basle. In retirement Lieutenant-Colonel Sterckx has been involved in editorial and translation work for the Switzerland, Austria and Hungary Territory.

The Burning Bush

'I have indeed seen the misery of my people . . . I have heard them
crying out . . . I am concerned about their suffering.
So I have come down' (vv. 7, 8).

Exodus has been called 'the book of redemption' – and redemption tells us that God comes with grace towards mankind. His approaches are many and, as we see in today's reading, not immediately understood. He comes to his chosen man, Moses, in a fire in a bush and speaks through an angel. An angel, a bush not burning up – how strange! By what means could Moses ever know that God is there? Does he know God at all, in fact?

What Moses sees is no usual spectacle in the midst of a desert, so he takes a closer look. A voice calling his name stops him; he should take off his sandals. The reason given: this is holy ground.

Through the fire that does not burn up the bush, God identifies himself as the Unchanging One. Then he reveals his plans to his chosen partner. God tells Moses of his promises to the patriarchs and links the puzzled shepherd to the long-prepared redemption plan. Salvation is God's central message and compassion its motivation. Moses is to be part of it. The divine message given to Moses will now be part of his whole future life.

God's message begins with an 'I', and it captures Moses' thinking. Here the Lord God who is and remains the first person speaks: 'I am the God of your father; I have seen; I have heard; I am concerned; I have come; I will send you; I will be with you; it is I who has sent you; I am who I am.' I am who I am: God possibly means, 'I will be what I will be' – which is summed up with the four Hebrew letters JHWH. My French Bible frequently uses *L'Eternel* (the Eternal One) when naming God.

Moses' instinctive sense of awe comes upon us too. We cannot escape it in our encounters with our Lord. Therefore let us have some holy restraint when we come to meet the Holy One. Likewise, let us remember that in Christ we come to the Father! We pray with a reverent awe balanced with an unlimited trust.

Knee Drill in Gilgal

' "What message does my Lord have for his servant?" . . . "Take off your sandals, for the place where you are standing is holy." And Joshua did so'
(vv. 14, 15).

God is very near again. In this second theophany, God comes towards Joshua as near as he came when he met Moses. For Moses, the appearance was to reveal a transcendent God, his nature, his love, his unchanging plan of salvation. In his revelation to Joshua the Lord shows the land he promised is a land to be possessed. It is a turning point in the Jews' own history and from now on the command is to conquer and occupy the land. It explains why the visitor who confronts Joshua is a man with a sword. The divine appearance calls himself 'the commander of the Lord's army'.

The apparition's attributes remind us of many Bible symbols such as the cherubim with a flaming sword in Genesis 3:24 and the son of man pictured in Revelation 1:16. Between these contrasting verses, we know about the weaponry in Ephesians 6:17 and the statement in Hebrews 13:8. We don't forget the double-edged sword of the messenger addressing the church in Pergamum (Revelation 2:12).

Why the sword? There is an enemy to resist and to overcome. The sword is a symbol of power needed for all the battles to be fought. Here is a sufficient explanation of the Lord's presence in the plains of Jericho. Here is a confirmation for Joshua that heaven and earth not only meet, but are now fighting together.

If God is there, then Joshua stands on holy ground. The battle against the Amalekites (Exodus 17:13) reminds him that he saw God in action before. There is no doubt about the victory for the battle to come; he has the Lord on his side. More than convinced and obedient, Joshua takes off his sandals and falls face down in an act of worship and submission.

We remember moments we can describe as holy instances of visitation. Wherever we were, God came to surround us with his holy care, his love and direction. Such blessed encounters are granted according to our circumstances and needs at the time they occur.

God's Intensive Care

'There by his head was a cake of bread . . . and a jar of water' (v. 6).

Heaven is very near whatever situations his people are in. How many of us have known God's tender grace in times of need? Here is a well-known episode: the prophet Elijah's burn-out and breakdown. Is it post-traumatic stress? How helpful is it to find such human situations in our Bible!

Elijah's situation has many causes: giving God's clear message of coming judgment, political and religious opposition, ups and downs in the task, times of dryness and hunger, awareness of the adversary's opposition and fear because of a death threat. Too much emotion, too much of everything!

Could burn-out after battle or maybe depression post-victory be the causes? Surely for our sake and information, the Bible clearly analyses Elijah's situation: fleeing for solitude, feeling useless, self-pity, complaining and even a death wish.

In the desert God gives intensive care: good food and good sleep. Later, after another long walk to God's mountain, further intensive care with more healing: the soft breeze, searching, loving questions and more divine instructions. Note here that God takes care of him before reminding him that the battle goes on.

Many of us experience some general weakness at times. We feel frail and burdened and ask for help. When this happens we may be blessed with listening ears and loving care, prayerful assistance from loved ones and friends in the faith and pastoral support, sometimes even medical help.

'My God will meet all your needs,' says Paul (Philippians 4:19). In this testimony he reminds us of a promise of provision when we come near exhaustion. Let's remember that we are body, soul and spirit. Through whatever channel, and whichever part his hand touches us, he does it as a loving Father and a divine doctor. As Annie Johnson Flint's hymn says:

> He giveth more grace as our burdens grow greater . . .
> To added afflictions he addeth his mercy,
> To multiplied trials he multiplies peace.
>
> (*SASB* 579)

Forgiveness After All

'You are to live with me . . . and I will live with you' (v. 3).

No failure is final. Today's reading contains two closely-knit life situations: Hosea's personal tragedy and Israel's apostasy. The book of Hosea brings a double message of hope, forgiveness, repair and healing – another human scene that shows how near God comes to us. He comes down in numberless ways and uses many channels to touch mankind's misery. Through the marriage distress of the prophet, God has words of patience and love that also translate his concern for his chosen people living in sin. The beauty of the book lies in the love claims of the betrayed husband as he conveys God's compassionate appeals.

At this time Jeroboam II is leader of the northern kingdom. His predecessor has led the people astray, worshipping idols. His true motivation was to prevent his countrymen from returning to Jerusalem for the Jewish festivals. In doing this he made Samaria with all its foreign cults the northern capital.

Hosea's central message is that the people have forsaken God. Verse 3 describes Israel's backsliding. As a result the nation is to be centuries without king, without temple, its altar and priests. The exile in Babylon in 536 BC and the Diaspora after AD 70 say how really the prophecy proved to be true.

Gomer's predicament tells the difficulty of a prostitute to return to a life of complete dignity with solid family support. Her damaged personality might cause Hosea and her children to suffer immensely, but the prophet's faith in God's redemption is unwavering. Through Hosea's forgiving gesture, Gomer recovers her true womanly destiny and place at home. Can a couple in such a distress and failure love again? To what extent does God heal wounds so deep? Hosea's story is proof enough for complete forgiveness, however difficult the path of repairs proves to be. This is the message of God's grace!

The patience of Hosea mirrors the patience of God. No failure is final in God's eyes! Redemption is a vessel overflowing with unconditional love. Hosea's book is another gospel.

Daniel's Unbending Decision

'Daniel resolved not to defile himself' (v. 8).

Two traps await Christians: a bitter persecution or a cosy way of life. In an address to Salvationists attending a Founders' Day celebration in Westminster Abbey, London, during The Salvation Army's centenary congress in 1965, General Frederick Coutts said: 'Make no mistakes. Beware when the world praises you . . . Make no mistakes and watch your steps because the devil may trap you at the next corner.' Not that the General wished the Army hard times, but he was not self-satisfied with its good reputation.

Young Daniel, along with his Jewish comrades, was Nebuchadnezzar's special guest in Babylon. It was then common for an invader to select young nobles or princes of the defeated land, remove them from their own country and offer them a kind of golden jail. The plan was to 'convert' these hostages into the local culture, customs and even religion. The process of depersonalisation already existed in those times.

What the Babylonians ignored was that God had a special eye on these boys (v. 9). Unknown to them, Daniel and his friends had faith in their God and were faithful to the Jewish principles. Strong was their religion, lasting was their engagement. No temple for worship, no Jewish festivals to celebrate, no bearings? They would set a strong spiritual course without it. Here is a lesson for us.

They took two important steps. Their resolve asked for a clear 'No!' to all that was doubtful, unclear and unclean. The Christian path always confronts us with such choices. They took their Lord along in the decision. It was challenging God – yes, very much so! (v. 8)

Much later, the prophet Malachi quotes God's calling out: 'Test me in this [faith in his provision] . . . and see if I will not throw open the floodgates of heaven and pour out so much blessing that you will not have room enough for it' (3:10). What an assurance there!

Birthplace of the Liberator King

*'But you, Bethlehem . . . out of you will come for me one who
will be ruler over Israel' (v. 2).*

Bethlehem was first noted in the Bible when Rachel was buried (Genesis 35:19). Later, it is the town Ruth settles in, and it goes on to feature through the story of David. Today, Bethlehem is situated on the West Bank, ten kilometres south of Jerusalem. After the creation of the state of Israel on 14 May 1948, United Nations Resolution 181 decided on borders that left Bethlehem away from the Hebrew state. Nevertheless, David's city has become an important religious site both for the practising Jews (Rachel's tomb) and for the Christians (the Shepherds Field and the Birth of Jesus Basilica). It is now partially surrounded by a defence wall built by the Jewish state.

Prophesying probably in the time of the Assyrian invasion, Micah speaks about a coming liberator (2:12–13) and the recovered position of Jerusalem (4:8), then moves on to announce the birthplace of this Liberator King. Micah 5:2 tells us about this birthplace.

When the wise men arrive in Jerusalem they have but little information. Did the law teachers from Jerusalem have any idea of their exact role as they indicated Jesus' birthplace? How well were they inspired in quoting Numbers 24:17, a mysterious prophecy: 'A star will come up out of Jacob, a sceptre will rise out of Israel'? Looking at the stars seemed to be the seekers' science but was a moving star attractive and exciting enough to get them moving on such a journey and follow this curiosity?

Looking for a king in Roman-occupied Jerusalem adds another question mark. The city of David should be the place, was the answer, so they moved south towards Bethlehem. Studying the stars made them heaven-minded and surely divinity-seekers. God had a reward for their search: they saw King Jesus.

We admire their act of faith. And the book of Jeremiah offers us a good epilogue for their story: 'You will seek me and find me when you seek me with all your heart' (29:13).

Small Beginnings (3):

Learn the Lessons

'I will utter things hidden since the creation of the world' (v. 35).

The parables of the mustard seed and the leaven formed a pair in Matthew's and Luke's Gospels. Both parables have the same essential point. If the mustard seed speaks of the growth of a tiny seed, the leaven describes the significant influence of a small amount of leaven mixed into the dough.

In both cases the kingdom of God is compared to the process involved. From small insignificant beginnings the reign of God will grow and its influence will be all-pervading. In his teaching of the leaven Jesus uses its influence in a positive way to make a point similar to that he makes through the mustard seed.

The first disciples at this point in the earthly ministry of our Lord were bewildered and discouraged. The opposition was becoming more intense. Jesus' teaching, with his call to self-surrender, obedience, servanthood, suffering and cross-bearing, was beginning to have an impact.

However, in both these parables Jesus is encouraging his disciples. Jesus is also saying to his twenty-first-century disciples, 'Be of good cheer, take heart.' These parables clearly teach that a process has commenced which must go on to its inevitable end. In spite of opposition, there will be a harvest and it will, says Jesus, be an abundant harvest.

Never despise small beginnings, especially when God is in them. Everyone has leaven in their lives. That is to say, every person exerts an influence, whether for good or for evil. Let us be encouraged. God is very much alive and working in his world today.

The dynamic ferment begun in Galilee 2,000 years ago is still spreading. The seed, which God gave Jesus to sow, is still growing. Christ's cause will prevail and his kingdom will triumph.

Adam's Heritage: Death
Christ's Heritage: the Resurrection Life

'Because of his great love for us, God, who is rich in mercy, made us alive with Christ even when we were dead in transgressions' (Ephesians 2:4, 5).

Consider the following quotations:

Cursed is the ground because of you; through painful toil you will eat of it all the days of your life. It will produce thorns and thistles for you and you will eat the plants of the field. By the sweat of your brow you will eat your food, until you return to the ground, since from it you were taken; for dust you are and to dust you will return. (Genesis 3:17–19)

If, by the trespass of the one man, death reigned through that one man, how much more will those who receive God's abundant provision of grace and of the gift of righteousness reign in life, through the one man, Jesus Christ. (Romans 5:17)

These two texts give some insight of what we, as Christians, endure because of our 'Adam heritage'. Eden is a place where heaven and earth could meet without any obstacle, and man knows fellowship with God. But ruptures occur and fellowship is broken with God, with mankind and with nature. The consequences? The first domestic quarrel, the first murder and a divorce with the earth.

Separation from God is the greatest evil. To illustrate this, Genesis 3:24 tells of a door that was shut, excluding not only Adam but every sinner of such fellowship. 'All have sinned,' comments Paul (Romans 5:12, 18–19) and all mankind will suffer eternal death if Jesus does not reopen this door. The good news of redemption is found in these affirmations: 'I am the door', 'the way . . . the life' (John 10:7, 14:6); 'As in Adam all die, so in Christ all will be made alive' (1 Corinthians 15:22); ' "The first man Adam became a living being"; the last Adam, a life-giving spirit' (v. 45).

Now rejoice with me in reading Revelation 4:1: 'After this I looked, and there before me was a door standing open in heaven.' The open door gives a way that leads us to heaven. We may return to dust because of Adam's heritage, but we shall live on because Jesus' life was granted to all who believe.

104

Do Not Pass Me By

'If I have found favour in your eyes, my lord,
do not pass your servant by' (v. 3).

Here we have a glimpse of history with a deep spiritual content. In this encounter the patriarch, Abraham, meets God's own envoys: Jewish tradition has identified the three visitors as Raphael, Michael and Gabriel whereas some scholars even imagine a foreshadowing of the Trinity. Who knows? Here is another example showing the heavenly plan fulfilled with and through human material.

With the visit of heaven's plenipotentiaries as messengers Abraham experiences hearing God again. Good news they bring: Abraham's long-awaited heir is announced. Mixed reactions are recorded here. The patriarch promptly offers hospitality to the three messengers, including refreshing rest and food, whilst he speaks this prayer: 'Do not pass your servant by.'

Sarah's reaction is more down to earth. Abraham's faith looks to God whilst his wife looks to herself, and her promised maternity is rather subject to caution. Let us not comment on Sarah's doubts. She is a realistic person after all! The message concerns the couple for a start but its outcome is greater in its scope. The couple's coming son is another sign of God's plan for the whole of mankind, another proof of the link existing between divinity and humanity, Abraham and Sarah being God's chosen instruments.

This story is prophetic: one day in God's agenda another promised seed shall be given; God's own Son will come as the greatest miracle. We read about this promise in Genesis 12:1–3.

Whether through this same story or through the existence of the Church, God never intended to act without his people. A logical consequence prompts us to pray: 'Lord, whatever you plan for the world in using your Church, do not pass us by!' And to that add Fanny Crosby's hymn:

> Pass me not, O loving Saviour, hear my humble cry;
> And while others thou art calling, do not pass me by.
> *(SASB* 301)

God Was There

'I am with you and will watch over you wherever you go' (v. 15).

Jacob too appears in Jesus' lineage. What makes this patriarch interesting is his second name: Israel. When considering his personal encounters with God, two locations are important: Bethel and Peniel. The first means 'house of God'; the second, 'face of God'.

Of Jacob's dream at Bethel many scholars mention a stairway that bridges the space between heaven and earth. Here is a picture of redemption where New Testament readers may see the foreshadowed cross bridging the gap between God and men. We see God and his heavenly companions, the angels, in full action proclaiming a message of grace.

As for the frightened fugitive, God takes him by surprise with the affirmation, 'I am the Lord' followed by God's assurance of descendants, God's extended blessing and his continuing presence. Jacob's only quick reaction shows awe as he acknowledges that God was there even when he did not know it. What seems to be a bargain with God is rather a way of taking the promise of verse 15 literally, from the general blessing to the more particular benefits.

'God was there and I didn't know' – what Jacob says may recall an experience we all have had. There are many occurrences when God acts without our awareness. It is enough for us to search in our memory to discover so many hidden blessings.

'God was there, and so was I,' Jacob should have said, since God's purpose is to confront this man with his true person. This took time. Between the Bethel and Peniel experiences almost twenty years elapse: years spent in gaining influence and power, searching for more wealth and beneficial relationships.

All this time Jacob treats people around from his own selfish desires. Attempting to change others demands needless energies – and Jacob tried a lot! Thomas à Kempis had a good formula: 'You cannot make others as you wish them to be since you cannot make yourself as you wish to be.' When Jacob reaches the brook at Peniel, he needs God's strong hand to change his ways: 'I saw God face to face,' he testifies, 'and yet my life was spared' (Genesis 32:30).

No Foreigner in God's Eyes

*'Praise be to the LORD, who this day has not left [us] without a kinsman-
redeemer' (v. 14, taken collectively).*

The book of Ruth is a delightful story planted in the midst of human-
knitted lives, where battle for living prevails. Hers is a family saga with
all the possible events life brings: struggle in times of hunger and poverty.
Yet there is belief in God in spite of bitter family dramas.

The book's four chapters picture an atmosphere of piety, love and
purity. In the midst of it all, coming out of the desert, there appears a
non-Hebrew woman from Moab. She knows little of God, yet shows
courage when facing many obstacles, and displays simple belief and
faithfulness. Her marriage to Boaz will make her a link in Jesus' genealogy
(v. 17). Three generations will come to pass before David appears in her
descendants. Boaz and Ruth will have a son, Obed – to become David's
grandfather.

The Hebrew race comes from the melting-pot of nations living in the
ancient Near East. Abraham and his wife were Chaldeans; Isaac and Jacob
marry Aramean women; Ephraim and Manasseh are the children of Joseph
and an Egyptian; Moses will marry an Ethiopian woman. The Bible shows
God caring for all people from all nations. Ruth's story is no exception.

At first, Ruth settling in Bethlehem may be seen as a problem for the
village. She is a foreigner, yet she will be soon integrated. Her piety needs
no facade. Everything in her new life is the outcome of the promise she
once made to Naomi her mother-in-law: 'Where you go I will go, and
where you stay I will stay. Your people will be my people and your God my
God. Where you die I will die, and there I will be buried. May the LORD
deal with me, be it ever so severely, if anything but death separates you and
me' (1:16–17).

In making this choice Ruth pays a great price: she leaves her house, her
land, her religion, her neighbourhood. Remember also that her story is
taken from the period of the judges. A general picture of the period shows
anarchy and apostasy in Israel, when God's word was forgotten (Judges
21:25).

The Lord God became Ruth's Lord – this was her choice. As a result of
her dedication, the blessing that came to her blossomed in many ways.

Indwelling and Authority when the Spirit Leads

'Man looks at the outward appearance, but the
LORD looks at the heart' (v. 7).

The explanation of Samuel's trip to Bethlehem can be found in two troubling verses: 'The Spirit of the LORD came upon David in power'; 'The Spirit of the LORD had departed from Saul' (vv. 13, 14). As we learn about the gift of God's Spirit, we see that in the Old Covenant it is granted for definite functions (prophet, priest, king). But one of King Saul's mistakes was to enjoy all the privileges and power of royalty, while forgetting the responsibilities. The prophet reacts to it and gives God's view of the king's doings (1 Samuel 15:22–23). Samuel has but a short preparation time for the next task: 'Take oil, and off you go where I send you!'

God's Spirit is very much at work in Samuel's ministry. Some similar impulses are to be found when Jeremiah is sent to the potter's house (Jeremiah 18:2), when Jesus goes into the desert (Matthew 4:1), when Philip is directed to the Gaza road (Acts 8:26) and when Ananias is sent to meet Saul (Acts 9:11). Today's servants may add their own experiences!

One of the outcomes of Pentecost is the much-needed gift of discernment (1 Corinthians 12:10) – the *NIV* uses the word 'distinguishing'. A lesson from Samuel's story shows how much we depend on first-sight conclusions. The prophet's sight proves too short for the decision needed to be made in Jesse's home. How can we be better partners without clear indications of God's plans and our obedience? This implicates closeness in prayer and an intimate communion to know and do God's will. Hesitation quickly gone, the last of the brothers – David – arrives as Samuel hears God's command: 'Rise and anoint him.'

We see the Spirit of God also mentioned in David's life of prayer. There is so much inspiration in his Spirit-filled poetry and songs, and of course in his repentance plea: 'Do not cast me from your presence or take your Holy Spirit from me' (Psalm 51:11). Then, as acknowledgment of God's omnipresence, we say with David: 'Where can I go from your Spirit?' (Psalm 139:7).

By God's Spirit Whatever the Task

'I deliberately kept it plain and simple: first Jesus and who he is; then Jesus and what he did – Jesus crucified' (1 Corinthians 2:2, MSG).

Here is another ancestor and not too well known. Nevertheless Zerubbabel is a link leading to Jesus. We find him in the time of the first returning contingent from the Babylon Exile under the leadership of Ezra the scribe. Haggai, Zechariah and Malachi are the main prophets of this time.

Who was Zerubbabel? His name may indicate that he was born in Babylon. He's the only person of royal blood in the time of this other 'exodus'. Another key person is Joshua the priest. The assembling of those three heads is of the utmost importance: scribe, priest and prince. They build an ideal headquarters.

This return is primarily a religious movement since the first activity is to rebuild the temple destroyed some seventy years before. Worth noting for personal reflection is that, under the supervision of Zerubbabel, the builders' tasks begin in restoring the altar (Ezra 3:2 and 68–69).

Haggai's prophecy calls Zerubbabel a signet of the Lord, chosen of him (Haggai 2:23). A signet is a seal printed to authenticate a document. This same word is also used to attest the authority of the Holy Spirit (Ephesians 1:13) and God's ownership on his servants (2 Corinthians 1:22). We may underline here how the Lord regards his servant: a holy man or woman chosen and entrusted with a holy task.

This definition takes us back to the building of the tabernacle in the desert and the construction of Solomon's temple: builders, too, were all filled by the Spirit of God (see Exodus 31:3). Their task was done in the midst of difficulties, disappointments and dangers. Those builders faced opposition, and therefore needed lots of encouragement. God's message of reassurance is timely and very much adapted to their condition, not to forget a warning about man-made tools: ' "Not by might nor by power, but by my Spirit," says the LORD Almighty' (Zechariah 4:6).

Yes, the same Spirit needs man's hands and, as we read in Zechariah 4:10, the same Spirit is found blessing the accomplishment of small things.

Courtroom Drama (1):

The Judge and a Widow

'Do not take advantage of a widow' (Exodus 22:22).

In first-century Palestine, widows traditionally were a vulnerable group. Girls regularly married at the young age of thirteen or fourteen years, often to men many years their senior. A widow, then, could well be quite a young person with no grown-up children to care for her. It is important to understand that the Old Testament places great importance upon the duty of treating widows and orphans with compassion and justice. For example, no one should wrong a widow.

Since this widow (the plaintiff in this court case) brings her grievance to a single judge and not before a tribunal, it would seem that the issue was one of finance. It is patently obvious that, in her appeal to the judge to give her justice, she has only one weapon in what is a hopeless cause – her courage and persistence, strengthened by the conviction of the justness of her cause.

In introducing the second of the two chief characters in this story – the judge – Jesus says he had no fear of God or respect for man (v. 2). One of the most negative criticisms possible of an adult in a Middle Eastern village is 'he does not feel shame'. Not a good character reference for the judge, and little encouragement for the just cause of this woman!

The judge had no spark of honour or compassion to which any plaintiff, least of all a helpless and vulnerable widow, could appeal. Like many of his colleagues, he would be prepared to listen if a suitable bribe was offered. Of course, the litigant was in no position to offer a bribe.

So then, the stage is set for a courtroom drama – a war of attrition between the two chief characters of our Lord's parable. Says the judge: 'This woman is such a nuisance that I shall give judgment in her favour, or else her continual visits will be the death of me!' (v. 5, *JBP*). Concluding his story, Jesus says: 'Do you suppose God, patient as he is, will not see justice done for his chosen, who appeal to him day and night?' (v. 7, *JBP*).

Incarnation is Everything in Christianity

'The Word became flesh and made his dwelling among us' (v. 14a).

John's prologue is like a musical prelude: a foretaste of all the tunes assembled in his work by the composer. These opening verses in John's Gospel form one of the richest parts of the New Testament. When John the Evangelist writes down the sentence recorded in verse 14, it is as though his whole Gospel revolves around this phrase. Its truth is restated and reaffirmed in a closing chapter: 'These [words] are written that you may believe that Jesus is the Christ, the Son of God, and that by believing you may have life in his name' (20:31). The Christian faith is anchored in that belief and based upon the proclaiming of the incarnation. Indeed, it is a faith affirmation that the whole New Testament comes to support.

Paul confirms this as he writes that Christ, 'being in very nature God, did not consider equality with God something to be grasped, but made himself nothing, taking the nature of a servant, being made in human likeness . . . in appearance as a man' (Philippians 2:6–8). The same truth appears in John's first letter: 'Every spirit that acknowledges that Jesus Christ has come in the flesh is from God' (4:2).

Those words are faith-sustaining for all who believe. If faith in God can transform human beings born of the flesh, it is because that faith is built upon this great truth: 'the Word became flesh'!

It isn't easy thinking, but the coming to faith of the first disciples may help us. They were Jews, they followed Jesus, but to believe he was God's Son and their Messiah took time. They heard him preach and teach, saw the miracles he performed, but they had to witness that their Lord was rejected and crucified. As John states (2:22), the resurrection and Pentecost were necessary stages so that their faith would grow.

So, back to John's letter: 'From the very first day, we were there, taking it all in – we heard it with our own ears, saw it with our own eyes, verified it with our own hands. The Word of Life appeared right before our eyes; we saw it happen! And now we're telling you . . . what we witnessed was, incredibly, this: 'The infinite Life of God himself took shape before us' (1 John 1:1–2, *MSG*).

111

The Word Became Flesh – 'At-one-ment'?

'The Word became flesh and blood, and moved into the neighborhood'
(John 1:14a, MSG).

There's no Christmas story in John's Gospel, but our key verse replaces it in full. 'Forget this verse', said a rabbi teaching officer cadets in The Salvation Army's training college in Switzerland, 'and all your New Testament falls into pieces!' No other religion has such a statement. God reaches and touches our humanity, and we grasp the meaning of the word 'atonement'. He redeems lost mankind as he comes to be one with us. Yes, God and man become one from that moment on.

The verb 'became' linked to 'the Word' hides a difficulty here. How could the divinity leave a kind of celestial state in heaven and get dressed and wear our material body with the limitations of space and time? Perhaps the Old Testament can give some help here. Exodus 25:8 has this prophetic analogy: 'Make a sanctuary for me and I will dwell among [you].' Didn't Jesus mention the same sanctuary, but this time speaking of himself and addressing the sign-seeking Jews? 'Destroy this temple, and I will raise it again in three days,' he said (John 2:19).

Does the description, 'this temple', fit a celestial appearance in a human dress? God chooses the most unlikely manner to appear in our world. There, in a manger lies a newborn refugee baby, naked and fragile, his breathing already threatened by the evil world he comes to. What kind of revelation is this? And how far we are from heaven! But this is God's own Son and his breathing has its source in the divine breath. The manger is nothing like a holy place, true. But this is creation revisited and here is the divine paradox: the New Covenant is being signed there.

Body and flesh take us once more to Paul's writings. When the New Testament mentions the flesh, it includes the whole being as in 1 Thessalonians 5:23. The flesh encompasses everything that we are: body, soul, spirit. The incarnate Christ we worship is fully described in those three words! By faith, the whole nature of Jesus encounters mine. This is holiness: a blessing granted to all believers.

God's Typography: the Word Spelled
with Words

'The word of God became a human being and lived among us'
(John 1:14, JBP).

A French version of our key verse says: 'The language entered a body.' When God reveals himself then the issue is a language, a communication: 'In the beginning was the Word' says the opening of John's prologue, and all through the Scriptures God speaks. It can be compared with a mighty projector's beam aimed at his Word. The Holy Spirit confirms it, translating God's message for our understanding.

Capturing God's language should develop into communication. A little help to enrich this word comes from the Italian language: communication and communion both come from *come uno* ('as one'), leading to union or reunion. Talking with God never meant monologue. The Word's divine metamorphosis offers and provokes dialogues.

'Dialogue' is also an interesting word. Split the word in two (*dia-logos*) for it to mean a communication breakthrough. Real dialogue meets and overcomes obstacles. This is clearly shown in the redemption story. God's word is like a sharp and piercing sword attacking all our silences and the causes of them (see Hebrews 4:12). Yes, God's word keeps coming to us and it is a constant breakthrough.

The first searching question in the Bible is: 'Where are you?' (Genesis 3:9). The Lord called out to the man and awaited his response. To later generations the prophets' complaint is: 'I called but you did not answer, I spoke but you did not listen' (Isaiah 65:12); 'I spoke to you again and again, but you did not listen; I called you, but you did not answer' (Jeremiah 7:13). The writer of the letter to the Hebrews begins with: 'In the past God spoke to our forefathers through the prophets at many times and in various ways', then adds: 'but in these last days he has spoken to us by his Son' (1:1–2). God's language entered a body.

God Could Not Come Any Closer

*'I have brought you glory on earth by completing the work
you gave me to do' (v. 4).*

When John writes, 'The Word . . . made his dwelling among us' he chooses a term campers know. In New Testament vocabulary the same Greek term also indicates a limited stay (see 2 Peter 1:13–14). So camping may help us to read John 1:14 as the incarnated Word 'set up his tent close to ours'. What a tremendous statement!

To complete the verb 'dwelling', and to paint a clearer picture of Jesus, the New Testament uses a name that indicates both his divine and human origin: Emmanuel (God is with us and on our side). Imagine Jesus' companions giving the following testimony after his ascension: 'We ate and drank together, slept under the same roof, walked and travelled together, sailed together. We saw him as son, brother, friend; guest of Pharisees and publicans. We saw him withdrawing for prayer, we watched him as he spoke to God as his Father. We observed our Master as he remained faithful to his divine mission, while living in his chosen human life.'

For the twelve, Jesus' human nature had more consequences. Their Master shared their weariness on many occasions. He was seen weeping over a friend's death. He endured criticism and remained silent in front of false accusations. Left alone by some followers, he was rejected. Finally, his body was cruelly beaten. Here was the heavy price paid for his humanity. Therefore his Spirit-baptism at the Jordan was not a mere sacred rite: the Holy Spirit was to be his much-needed ever-present daily companion.

The same empowering Holy Spirit came upon the disciples as promised by their Master. Then the word 'indwelling' appears again and means 'anointing' (1 John 2:20, 27). Behind these words is the expression, 'being filled by the Spirit'. His dwelling – or indwelling – is an experience offered to all believers. God is close and he could not be any closer. God's nearness is granted for our sake: 'He [the Holy Spirit] lives with you and will be in you' (John 14:17). May we all find our longings satisfied!

Seeing His Glory

*'We have seen his glory, the glory of the One and Only [Son],
who came from the Father' (John 1:14b).*

At the beginning of this verse, John chooses an Old Testament word and he attaches it to belief in the incarnation. His word is a key word: the glory. Where does it take us, if not to wonder at and to witness a celestial display? We could describe it as 'beholding the glory'.

The Bible reader will have no difficulties finding references to the glory, although to define it may not be easy. We read about a shining presence, an atmosphere dense and intense, almost invading – a divine manifestation leaving human beings filled with awe. We may be helped by accounts of the dedications of the tabernacle and the temple, when God's glory fills those places (Exodus 40:34; 1 Kings 8:11).

God's holiness is there in such fullness, it is humanly unbearable – to the point that the priests have to remain outside, keeping a safe distance. But no separation remains any more when John mentions the same glory embodied in Christ. The New Testament invites us to approach freely God's new temple on earth (John 2:21; Hebrews 10:19–22) and to share the glory that shines there.

In writing 'we have seen his glory', John probably recalls the transfiguration (Luke 9:32). But the glory mentioned by John the Evangelist has little to compare with the glory the Son possessed before the incarnation. It is the same glory that Jesus is asking in his prayer: 'And now, Father, glorify me in your presence with the glory I had with you before the world began' (John 17:5).

Can this glory be seen in us? Yes! This glory reflects our communion with our Master, our life of holiness, our testimony, the words of wisdom spoken and all the deeds accomplished in his name, visible or not. In short, all that shines and all that reproduces Christ living in us deserves this description. As Paul says: 'We, who with unveiled faces all reflect the Lord's glory, are being transformed into his likeness with ever-increasing glory, which comes from the Lord' (2 Corinthians 3:18).

The Fullness of His Grace, Costly and Pure

*'Grace, mercy and peace from God the Father and from Jesus Christ, the
Father's Son, will be with us in truth and love' (2 John 3).*

Cheap grace, says Dietrich Bonhoeffer in his book, *The Cost of
Discipleship*, is the worst enemy of the Church. Cheap grace, he states,
is grace wrapped in religious systems and doctrines. It is the automatic
forgiveness of sins becoming universal truth; it is the love of God
becoming a Christian idea about God; it is justification of sin instead of
justification of the sinner.

Grace is costly. Paul says it has cost God a great price, the life of his Son
(1 Corinthians 6:20). And grace lay at the roots of reformation, Martin
Luther pointing out that the gospel of Christ is a gospel of grace – a pure
and costly grace, he affirms again and again.

Further in John's prologue we read that if 'the law was given through
Moses, grace and truth came through Jesus Christ' (John 1:17). As Paul
was travelling through Galatia he had to fight what he called 'another
gospel' and probably the apostle John had known about it. To describe the
problem briefly, so-called apostles were preaching a 'gospel after Moses'
(Galatians 2:1–5, 3:1–5).

The line drawn between law and grace was always tenuous: cheap
grace on one side and expensive grace on the other – neither reflecting the
good news. Everyone tending God's flock knows it, and leadership
decisions require much of God's gift of discernment. Happily John speaks
eloquently about the grace of God. So eloquently, that he adds the word
'fulness' to it (John 1:16).

I recall an illustration given by the late Belgian archbishop, Leo
Suenens. He said the grace of God is like a fountain where plenty of fresh
and pure water flows abundantly. Sadly, we come to drink using only a
thimble!

What about us? Think of when we need renewed grace. This grace is
available; it overflows time and again from God's heart. Look at verse 16:
it is from grace we receive blessing after blessing. So, as Peter writes, 'set
your hope fully on . . . grace' (1 Peter 1:13).

Courtroom Drama (2):

A Matter of Priority

'Then Jesus told his disciples a parable to show them that they should always pray and not give up' (v. 1).

The audience for this story is made clear in the opening verse; the parable is concerned with teaching disciples of Jesus. The central theme and focus is found in this key verse. *The Message* paints a graphic word picture in its free paraphrase of the verse: 'Jesus told them a story showing that it was necessary for them to pray consistently and never quit.'

The Greek word for 'never lose heart' is *enkakein*. It has the meaning that the disciple of Christ must never 'get fed up' with praying. Consider just two examples of the importance and priority of prayer, in particular, intercessory prayer, for the follower of Christ: 'You must never stop praying' (1 Thessalonians 5:17, *WB*); 'Constantly ask God's help in prayer, and pray always in the power of the Spirit. To this end keep watch and persevere, always interceding for all God's people' (Ephesians 6:18, *WB*).

As we reflect on this parable, let us be encouraged and challenged to make prayer, especially intercessory prayer, a vital part of our Christian lifestyle. Most of us find that prayer does not come naturally. In fact, if we are honest with ourselves, we will need to confess that we do not pray enough. This impoverishment of prayer, both for the individual and the Christian community, has been further diminished by the impact of the materialistic, technological Western society upon our minds and lifestyle.

In what is a very complex subject, one point is clear – the great need to realise that the heart of mission and ministry is communion with God, even in the midst of the world's noise and demented activism.

Prayer is the very lifeblood of mission. It is not something one does, it is a style of living. The prayer I am speaking of is the prayer of silence. It is essentially a form of intercession, and as such is completely spontaneous and therefore gives God the Holy Spirit a chance to suggest whom and what we should pray for.

Prayer Was Heard

'He will be an instrument for noble purposes, made holy, useful to the Master and prepared to do any good work' (2 Timothy 2:21).

After four centuries of prophetic silence God speaks. From now on, whether through the life of his Son or through the Church, mankind will hear his voice. Luke's description of this old couple shows divinity and humanity alike. First their names have meaning. The priest's name means 'The Lord remembers' and Elizabeth means 'God's oath'. The evangelist adds a description of their faith, their blameless testimony and their faithful observance of the Jewish cult.

Zechariah's sacred task has to do with the incense burning in the Holy Place and this is the reminder of permanent intercessory prayers rising to God. When this rite is fulfilled, God's angel Gabriel appears to the priest and surprises him. Is he a reluctant believer? He is afraid, to say the least. The first words from Gabriel are full of peaceful reassurance. The same calming words will be said to Mary (Luke 1:30) and to the shepherds on Bethlehem's hills (2:10).

There is a message for the shaken priest: the long-expected son is announced. Zechariah questions the angel to be sure (1:18). They will give birth to a child whose name is already chosen. Like Elijah, the son will be a Spirit-filled instrument of God's redemption. We all understand wavering belief, but this is not unbelief. Nonetheless God gives his servant a warning sign for his faith: until the birth of the baby, Zechariah will be kept silent.

A many times proven fact: God knows where to look for faithful people to serve his plans and the kind of servants he chooses to fulfil them. This old couple is nothing but very fertile soil. All the Lord's plans require simple obedience from dedicated servants. Zechariah, Elizabeth and later John enter in this preparation. Not just any preparation: a heaven-prepared Christmas.

We owe Luke a lot for recording the four songs associated with the birth of Jesus. The *Benedictus* (Latin: 'blessing'!) is the first. This is a psalm of praise. It celebrates the Lord: his mercy, his great salvation and his glory.

My Eyes Have Seen God's Salvation

'He remembers his covenant for ever, the word he commanded,
for a thousand generations, the covenant he made with Abraham'
(Psalm 105:8–9).

Here we read the *Nunc Dimittis* ('Now let me go'), the fourth Christmas song recorded in Luke, and not the least although shorter than the first three. Note the wealth of our text.

Luke often mentions the presence and the action of the Holy Spirit in his Gospel (and in the book of Acts). Simeon is guided inside the temple courts by the Holy Spirit with the same impulse and indwelling that has kept him attached to the Old Testament prophecies. Later, the same command will direct Philip the evangelist to meet the Ethiopian (Acts 8:29).

Simeon is an eye-witness that God's promise was true. He is another chosen servant amongst the most humble people to see Jesus. Joy, hopes fulfilled, intense satisfaction and peace – words are too weak to describe his experience. In his prayer Simeon even calls himself a slave, whose aim was to await the coming of the Messiah. As he contemplates the couple and the baby, light and understanding fill his heart. Here, clearly pointed to by the Holy Spirit, is the promised Redeemer.

Praise then flows from the old man's heart. God's salvation has come both for Israel and the nations (Luke 1:31–32). The good news is embodied; God has stayed true to his word. The heavens meet humanity; through the coming of Jesus a door is reopened: the promised light has come. In a way creation is being repeated. Now the only remaining wish for Simeon is to be with God. His prayer asks for his discharge.

But first Simeon links his words with Isaiah 7:14, where the word 'sign' is already used concerning Mary: 'This child is destined to cause the falling and rising of many in Israel, and to be a sign that will be spoken against so that the thoughts of many hearts will be revealed' (Luke 2:34–35). But what a strange and fearful statement is next for Mary! With a few words, Simeon adds a terrible prophecy to the glorious promises received at the time of the annunciation. The coming of the kingdom shall one day cost the King's life. For us all, as it was for Simeon then, the same Spirit is today guiding us – and anyone – towards Christ.

Glory to God, Peace on Earth!

*'You have hidden these things from the wise and learned,
and revealed them to little children' (Luke 10:21).*

As God's angel appears to the shepherds, the heavens cover the hills with light. No more sleep. Those men are awake. No more night since the glory of the Lord illuminates all around. No more silence since there is plenty of music and a proclamation. This is Christmas night. On this night God speaks through his angels and reveals himself. He grants those simple witnesses the unique privilege of contemplating a sky full of angelic songsters singing the 'Gloria', and giving them a solemn responsibility of telling all the people what they heard – good news to proclaim.

No Christians should ever imagine a gospel proclamation without song! I believe Jesus sang a lot; he would sing the psalms used for Jewish festivals. Think too of the severely beaten Paul and Silas preaching the gospel in Philippi's jail with songs of praise (Acts 16:25).

For the very simple shepherds the message with its glorious simplicity is the coming to earth of their Messiah, Lord and Saviour. They will know where and how to find him. Their reaction to this is prompt: 'Let's go and see!' Here is the first example of the 'communion of believers' at work: they unite and go.

After seeing the manger and the child they return to their world and testify, which gives us the example of the first evangelisation by lay people with its urgency and necessity. 'They hurried off . . . they spread the word . . . praising God.' Something very important occurs and causes their praise. They notice the perfect harmony between what they are told and what they see. Here is faith rewarded, grounded and enriched!

The Christmas shepherds represent the kind of believers Jesus mentions in Luke 10:21 – 'Father . . . you have . . . revealed [these things] to little children' – and I also like to see the shepherds as witnesses of God's salvation. We expect today's shepherds/pastors to proclaim the same plain salvation with watchful eyes, clear voices and caring ministries for the wellbeing of the communities entrusted to them.

The Servant Behind the Curtain

'Become the kind of container God can use to present any and every kind of gift to his guests for their blessing' (2 Timothy 2:21, MSG).

Nativity paintings often show Joseph as an old man. I rather see him as a younger person, a responsible and enterprising man who loves Mary dearly. Mary's fiancé needs to be discovered. His part in the nativity cast is essential and indispensable, since by birth he belongs to the house and the line of David, and is thus of royal descent. This will cause him and Mary to obey a Roman decree and travel from Galilee to Bethlehem to register. It shall be the birthplace of Jesus.

If there is a sample of humanity in the Christmas story, Joseph's part offers one. First he will welcome Mary in her pregnancy. The virgin has entrusted nothing less than her reputation to God's own care, and Joseph accepts this. A divine messenger confirms the miracle, and Joseph believes this. Without fully understanding the situation, he submits and follows the divine plan.

Four times in Matthew's Gospel we read that God's angel gives Joseph instructions through dreams. The evangelist records them: 1:20, 2:13, 2:19 and 2:22. Each time we discover that Joseph reacts as a protective husband and father – the picture of a faithful servant behind the scenes, obedient to the whole revelation and trustworthy in the extreme. Even believing the unbelievable, he displays practical faith. With Mary and the baby, he travels to Jerusalem's temple to present the child and fulfil the Jewish law and tradition of circumcision and an offering required for any firstborn male (Luke 2:21). Following the angel's instructions (Matthew 1:21), the name given is Jesus.

I admire Joseph as a humble but responsible family man, and not lacking parental authority and care (Luke 2:48). According to Matthew and Mark he is a working man: a carpenter. Joseph's life also fills a gap between the Old Testament and the New. He is one of the many instruments used by God in the redemption story – no weak link at all!

Answering the Many 'Hows' of Believers

'He who has an ear, let him hear what the Spirit says to the churches'
(Revelation 2:11).

The whole Christian Church owes three major Scripture texts to Mary: her question to the angel Gabriel and its answer; then the song of the 'Magnificat'; finally her statement at the marriage at Cana.

The annunciation question is the shortest conceivable – 'How?' How will this be possible? By what means? How can it happen? And what about the unique answer given to the universal Church? The angel recalls for Mary's benefit the long-foretold promise: 'The Holy Spirit will come upon you' (Ezekiel 37:14; Joel 2:28). Within a short suite of words the dialogue between the angel and the young woman sends us to the very nucleus of our credo: the incarnation.

It could not be simpler. Sadly, the Church has often complicated its fulfilment. Yet, it's such a grand promise! And it reminds us that 'Christ living in me' is more than a possibility, it is God's will. Paul's prayer for the Galatians confirms that the same miracle can be performed in us (Galatians 4:19).

The Holy Spirit is already felt in Mary's song (Luke 1:46–55). God is placed in the centre of her life as well as the world's destiny. God is glorified and Mary rejoices because her own life will serve his glory.

'Do what he says' seems to be her recommendation to all who serve at Cana – and anywhere in the world through the centuries afterwards. This again is spiritual advice. The Holy Spirit always redirects us to the person of Jesus (John 16:14).

Whatever the task and the need, Gabriel's answer encompasses us all. God is to be glorified in the Church and in every disciple's life. Obey Christ and his word, and submission to his lordship will be the logical outcome.

During my service in Italy, I discovered that the city of Rome has more than 600 churches all celebrating the virgin Mary. It is about her that the prophet Isaiah gives a sign – intended for Israel first, then for the confessing Church: 'The virgin will be with child and will give birth to a son, and will call him Immanuel' (Isaiah 7:14).

Heavenly Equipment to Serve on Earth

'But a body you prepared for me' (v. 5).

This may be an unusual text to consider on Christmas Eve, but it culminates all the New Testament teaching and it contains the greatest biblical truth for all believers. Jesus is Son of God and Son of Man. Few books in the Bible emphasise his deity and his humanity as clearly as this epistle does. Our passage gives the substance of a dialogue between the Father and the Son.

The writer of the epistle first quotes Psalm 40:6–9 and then as a New Testament incarnation assessment adds: 'A body you prepared for me'. The verb used here could indicate the human outfit the Father gave the Son for his coming on earth.

Do we understand that Christmas is God coming down for this very purpose: a new creation, but in a redemptive creation through Christ? If so – and the above verse in full has this additional meaning – no more sacrifices are required since Jesus' giving away his life equals and replaces all Jewish sacrifices.

It helps us to remember that this letter is written to the Hebrews and that the whole letter points towards their Messiah, Jesus. It is helpful to see Jesus appearing in the successive chapters. For instance: there are Old Testament saints – but the Son of God, Jesus, is greater than the Old Testament saints; there is the covenant of Mount Sinai – but the covenant signed at the cross completes it; there is the temple – but Jesus assembles in his person and deity all that it stands for, because he himself is the new temple. He is also the greatest high priest and the unique sacrifice. Think of forgiveness at Yom Kippur – through faith in God's salvation we are forgiven and justified. Yes, this letter is really the gospel written for the people of Israel.

Contemplate the manger scene and meditate on this word: incarnation. It is more than a religious word: it is God in Christ, God with us. Let the Holy Spirit illuminate Christmas. Then leave the Bethlehem stable, meet God at Calvary and worship the Risen Lord.

When Angels Spell the Word 'Christmas'

'Glory to God in the highest, and on earth peace to men' (v. 14).

The twofold affirmation of the angels gives the perfect 'amen' to the announcement of the coming Christ and his salvation, and their intimate and inseparable connection: giving God all glory and bringing the peace for all mankind (v. 14).

Manifesting God's glory is the sacred task given to all Christians. It means nothing less than the Church pulls heaven down upon our world. But is it really so? One of the dark marks of humanity is original pride and therefore we tend to miss our goal and usurp the glory that belongs to God. This is universal sin, with the consequence that fellowship with him is broken.

Old Testament books say a lot about God's glory departing the temple caused by a backsliding priesthood. God could not inhabit the holy place any more and refused to share his house with sin (Ezekiel 10). But as a result of the Son's obedience, the cross and victory over Satan, God is glorified again. The angels' song proclaims with power that the birth of Jesus celebrates the return of the glory.

In Matthew 22:21 we read, 'Give to . . . God what is God's.' So let us declare: 'Give glory to God and peace will come for mankind' – for only when God reigns can peace return. We know there are many Bible references to peace. For example, Isaiah calls Christ the Prince of Peace (9:6). Jesus promises and assures peace in times of trouble (John 14:1). He comes as the Risen Lord in the upper room to meet his frightened disciples with a greeting of peace (John 20:19). Paul describes peace as a fruit of the Spirit (Galatians 5:22).

So let us hear the angels' song as an exhortation. In the midst of all the Christmas feasts, family rejoicings and activities of all kinds, enjoy God's peace. Sense something of his glory in these days. Contemplate Jesus the King of kings.

Gifts

A post-Christmas series by Major Beverly Ivany

Introduction

As a prelude to her first edition of *Words of Life* as its new writer, Major Beverly Ivany provides comments for the days leading up to the new year. Beverly writes:

> Some of us receive many gifts at Christmas – often more than we really need. Others receive very few; but the ones received are treasured. But there is more to this beautiful season than the accumulation of physical gifts. God gives to each of us gifts that sometimes we might take for granted; gifts that could go unnoticed; ones that we might fail to recognise as treasures.
>
> A few of these special gifts are mentioned here. May we value them, and see them as gifts we can potentially share with others. As the year 2011 comes to a close, let us give thanks to God for the gift of life itself!

The Gift of Joy

'I have no greater joy than to hear that my children are
walking in the truth' (v. 4).

The gifts we receive at Christmas are wonderful; precious reminders that we are loved. Even if we only receive one or two gifts from others, they are treasured – for undoubtedly they are from people we cherish. But we also receive gifts that sometimes go unnoticed, or are not recognised. The gift of *joy* is one such gift.

Yes, we speak a fair bit about joy. And especially leading into Christmas, we sing about the joy of Christ's birth. Yet do we always internalise such joy for ourselves? Do we actually receive and acknowledge this same joy as a special God-given Christmas gift?

Having joy is something far deeper than having happiness. We actually choose to live with joy when it is offered to us, when it is recognised as a gift. We can look back over the past year. No doubt there have been struggles, even very difficult moments. Yet also, there have been moments of joy, yes? Above all it is the realisation that God has been present, imparting his joy for each of us.

How is this joy realised? What brings joy into our lives, this treasured gift from God? Perhaps it's as simple as a glorious sunrise; a morning stroll in our neighbourhood; the smell of a flower; a child's hand in ours; a glass of cold water; a conversation with a good friend; a smile from a stranger. God reveals himself in new and wonderful ways, daily. He likes to surprise us!

Joy. What a marvellous word! What a magnificent gift received! Say the word. Say it again. Breathe it in. Smile as you are saying it. Lift your head heavenward, thanking God for the gift of joy. And today, show this gift to others – without saying a word. Then feel free to sing and speak, giving evidence of the joy deep down in your heart. Play with a toddler. Listen to someone who needs an attentive ear. Live out God's joy in every possible way. For indeed, joy is a blessing. It's a gift to be shared with others today, and all the days to follow!

The Gift of Relationships

'There is a friend who sticks closer than a brother' (v. 24).

The gift of relationships received from God at Christmas is crucial for our faith. At the core, life is not about things; it's about our relationship with others. For each relationship determines the quality of life we live, day to day. They virtually show us who God is on earth. Relationships, when good and wholesome, enrich us like nothing else. Truly, they are a gift from God Almighty.

Our relationship with God is paramount. This vertical relationship is crucial; for it is at the centre of all we do, all we are. It's what holds everything else together. It must stay strong, solid and vibrant – for it is foundational. God invites us into relationship with himself. What a gift! How extraordinary to know Creator God wants us to commune with him, daily. It's hard to comprehend, really; difficult to take it all in.

Then, he graciously gives to us the opportunity of relationship with others. The horizontal relationships. Family, friends, potential friends. They turn the mundane into gold, for they are the alchemy of life. They make community a reality. They are indeed a sign of the presence of God in everyday living. For there is no such thing, at any stage of human development, as life without the gift of relationships. They bring new moments in time, new meaning to life, new awareness of God.

It is vital that we use this gift to the full, inviting people into our sphere. Older people, younger people; people similar to us, people very different from us. For each relationship opens new conversations; opportunities to go deep, to ponder the important things life presents to us.

Today, let's deepen the relationship we have with the Lord, by practising silence and solitude. But also, with God's help, let's try to establish brand new relationships. Let us reach out, beyond our own comfort areas, and explore all the possibilities. In doing this, we will bring great joy to the heart of God!

The Gift of Mystery

'Beyond all question, the mystery of godliness is great' (v. 16).

We have all just witnessed and have been intimately connected with another Christmas season. Yet still, we can never really grasp the significance and mystery of the incarnation, can we? In our hearts, we believe it to be absolute truth and reality; yet our finite minds wrestle with putting it all together. However, we are not meant to comprehend it all; to grasp the miracle of Christ's birth. Why is this so?

It is the gift of mystery, given to us for a purpose. It allows God's children to be part of him in a beautiful way. We are all included in this mystery; yet we cannot grasp why we have been chosen by him, to be used for his glory. And on top of all this, we have the knowledge that we are personally loved by Creator God. Amazing!

There is purpose to mystery, for it takes us into another realm. Most today live and exist in a carefully calculated, detailed world. Everything is timed; and the timing of everyday life can become routine, even mundane. Yes, we all need certain structure, various schedules; sometimes deadlines and time-lines are a necessity, in order to exist in society itself. But when these things come to rule our lives completely, they can consume us – squeezing out any possibility for something extraordinary to take place.

Mystery is what happens when we allow life to evolve, rather than consistently trying to make life happen. Mystery is freeing our souls to something new; a different smell, a different taste, a smile for someone we don't know. It's all about connections being made. Mystery is a breathless moment of astonishment, sensing God's presence. It takes us into a whole new awareness of the immanence of God.

What will happen today? Who will we meet today? What, today, will suddenly make our souls mysteriously leap for joy?

Thought

> **'O the wonder of it all!'**
> (George Beverly Shea, *Happiness and Harmony* 68, chorus³)

Gift of Time

*'There is a time for everything, and a season for every
activity under heaven' (v. 1).*

Time is a precious commodity, for it is truly a gift given by God. Today is a new day, and we can never take the time given to us each day for granted. And so, today, what will we do with our time? How much time will we spend alone with God and with reading his word? How much time with family, friends, reaching out to others?

Time ages things. It ages our memories, allowing us to reflect on the year that has just passed. The good times that took place, that brought a real sense of joy and fulfilment; and even the more difficult times, when there has been certain resolution, or healing.

Time deepens things. If we have spent time in God's word, we are better for it – have drawn closer to God. Friendships have no doubt deepened, for they have enriched us and blessed us. Perhaps we have intentionally been engaged in spiritual disciplines in a more intentional way. This time spent has drawn us closer to God. Our faith has become stronger; our love for the Lord has become richer.

Time ripens things. Throughout the past year, if we have been faithful servants, we have become more spiritually mature; we have become more accepting of others. We see greater opportunities for ministry, no matter what our age or situation. We are one step closer to the heavenly realm.

Time is a marvellous gift and we cannot afford to waste a moment of it. We must get off the treadmill of life, where we often find ourselves, and take time for more important things: time to spend with God in solitude and reflection; time for family; time to relax and walk and enjoy creation; time to read, play, exercise, help someone who is lonely; time to simply smell the roses. It will be time well spent – to enjoy the fullness of life God has given. Becoming . . . which takes time . . .

Today, will we spend every moment with the awareness that God is present? If we do, it will indeed be a glorious day!

Gift of the Present

'Give us today our daily bread' (v. 11).

Sometimes we live too much in the past. We reflect upon what happened way back; the good, and the not so good. At other times, we live too much in the future; the better job that might come, or the anticipated activities that could happen if this or if that takes place. What would benefit us more would be to accept, appreciate and value the gift of the present. The now. To make, with God's help, our lives count for something even more. To savour every moment. To relish all we have in the present – no matter how small or seemingly insignificant it may appear to be.

We are alive! Not just an existence, but alive in him! Do we feel the passion for life? For today is the first day of the rest of our lives. A brand new beginning. Not just another day. The present is to find a way into the centre of our souls, like never before. We are to take the manna, the bread, daily; for nourishment, for enjoyment, for sheer delight. For we don't know what tomorrow holds.

We don't even know if there will be a tomorrow, in fact. Thus, the sense of urgency – the kind that directs us to live fully in the present. For, wherever we find ourselves today, we realise each moment spent is a gift. We are to become acutely attuned to all that surrounds us.

There is power in the present, for it reminds us to value all we have. To see beauty in our world, in people. The present inundates us with life. Without the past, we couldn't live the present as we do. Without the present, lived fully for God, there will be no future.

Life is for living, now. The bread is for the present. Let's be thankful for what we have and live life to the full – for Christ's sake.

———————

Prayer

O Lord, thank you for the gift of the present. I want to live fully for you, fully engaged in all that happens – bringing you honour and praise. May I never take your bread for granted. I am yours. Show me your glory, today!

Gift of the Future

'Therefore do not worry about tomorrow, for tomorrow
will worry about itself' (v. 34).

What will the new year hold for us? Often, on the last day of the year, we reflect back to all that has taken place over the past months. But also, we are to live in anticipation of what is to come. The gift of the future. Tomorrow, and all the tomorrows to follow. Is there excitement in the air? Are we looking forward to what comes next?

The part of our lives to follow is to be lived to the full. God has so much in store for us. Do we trust him for the days that lie ahead, firmly believing we are in his hands – no matter what the future holds?

Perhaps it's finally time to let our spirits soar! To live life with complete abandonment; trusting him, for every moment of every day, for this coming year. For there is nothing stopping us, if our lives are in Christ. We are to live dangerously for him; to be fun-loving, to be fully engaged, to be totally alive.

As we anticipate the immediate future, no matter what stage we might find ourselves in life, there is nothing to hold us back from living life with an edge – even living on the edge. Living with strength, with energy, with complete freedom.

The future begins right away; and it is a cherished gift. Tomorrow is sacred. It will take care of itself, for God is already in the future. We are not to worry about it, even if the world would tell us that sickness or pain or difficulty should hold us back from trusting. With Christ beside us, and in us, the future will always be bright – ruling over all circumstances of life.

The future is for living life to the full. And life is to be cherished and enjoyed, beyond all measure. The future depends upon us, and our relationship with the Almighty. Let's anticipate it with thankful hearts. Let us rejoice in the giver of all gifts, Jesus Christ, our Lord and Saviour!

Notes

1. P. T. Forsyth, *The Person and Place of Jesus Christ* © 2006, Kessinger Publishing, Montana, USA.
2. C. H. Dodd, *The Parables of the Kingdom* © 1961, Collins, London, UK.
3. *Happiness and Harmony* © 1990 The General of The Salvation Army.

Index

Subscribe...

Words of Life is published three times a year:
January–April, May–August and September–December

Four easy ways to subscribe

- By post – simply complete and return the subscription form below
- By phone – +44 (0)1933 445 445
- By email – mail_order@sp-s.co.uk
- Or visit your local Christian bookshop

SUBSCRIPTION FORM

Name (Miss, Mrs, Ms, Mr)..

Address ....

....

.... Postcode ....

Tel. No..

Email* ....

Annual Subscription Rates
UK £10.50   *Non-UK* £10.50 + £3.90 P&P = **£14.40**
Please send me .... copy/copies of the next three issues of *Words of Life*
commencing with **January 2012**

Total: £ .... I enclose payment by cheque ☐
Please make cheques payable to *The Salvation Army*

Please debit my Access/Mastercard/Visa/American Express/Switch card

Card No. ☐☐☐☐ ☐☐☐☐ ☐☐☐☐ ☐☐☐☐   Expiry date: ___ /___

Security No. ☐☐☐ Issue number (Switch only) _____

Cardholder's signature: .... Date: ....

Please send this form and any cheques to: The Mail Order Department,
Salvationist Publishing and Supplies, 66–78 Denington Road, Denington
Industrial Estate, Wellingborough, Northamptonshire NN8 2QH, UK

☐ *We would like to keep in touch with you by placing you on our mailing list. If you would prefer not to receive correspondence from us, please tick this box. The Salvation Army does not sell or lease its mailing lists.